DISCARD

P9-EEU-796

How to Write Well in College

Alan Purves
University of Illinois

Sauli Takala
University of Illinois

Avon Crismore
University of Illinois

HARCOURT BRACE JOVANOVICH, PUBLISHERS
San Diego   New York   Chicago   Atlanta   Washington, D.C.
London   Sydney   Toronto

DISCARD

Austin Community College
Learning Resources Center

Copyright © 1984 by Harcourt Brace Jovanovich, Inc.

All rights reserved. No part of this publication may be reproduced or transmitted in any form or by any means, electronic or mechanical, including photocopy, recording, or any information storage and retrieval system, without permission in writing from the publisher.

Requests for permission to make copies of any part of the work should be mailed to: Permissions, Harcourt Brace Jovanovich, Publishers, Orlando, Florida 32887.

ISBN: 0-15-539370-7

Library of Congress Catalog Card Number: 83-82089

Printed in the United States of America

Copyrights and Acknowledgments begin on page 184, which constitutes a continuation of the copyright page.

Preface

We have written this book especially for you, the student who may be unsure about what kind of writing he or she will have to do in academic courses. As former students, and as teachers and researchers of writing today, we want to share with you some of the writing techniques we have learned and taught, so that you will gain confidence and learn to write well in college.

College is now your workplace. To avoid costly mistakes, you, like apprentices in any other workplace, need models to help you do your job well: We have chosen some readings similar to those you may encounter. These varied readings, along with the skills we will teach you and the practical exercises at the back of the book, will help you learn to examine what you read critically, to write about it efficiently, and to generate your own writing more easily.

Like an apprentice, you also need guidance in finding out what others will expect of you in the workplace: Individual instructors will have specific requirements — especially for writing assignments. Whereas most instructors agree on correct answers to math items, instructors often disagree about the acceptable way to write a paper or an essay exam. This book will help you learn how to integrate your instructors' requirements with your own writing goals, for you must learn to take control of the preparation and execution of your own writing.

Several skills which we teach in this book will help you accomplish both your instructors' requirements and your goals. First, since your instructors will emphasize in class those points they find important, learning to take meaningful notes from their lectures and from the books they require and recommend is essential. Second, once you have accumulated information, your task will be to organize and outline the materials you have gathered so that you can remember them and prepare them for extensive writing. Your third challenge will be to express what you have to say so that your instructor accepts your information as valid. You will learn methods of organization and development to make your writing coherent and convincing. You will also learn how you can use grammar effectively to make your writing concise and clear. Finally, we will show you how to individualize your writing with sound organizational methods.

Among the people who have influenced our work, we are especially indebted to George Dillon for *Constructing Texts: Elements of a Theory of Composition and Style* (Bloomington: Indiana University Press, 1981); Anneli Vähäpassi for "On the Domain of School Writing," *Studies in Educational Evaluation*, December 1982; Stanley Fish for *Is There a Text in This Class? On the Authority of Interpretive Communities* (Cambridge; Harvard University Press, 1980); Carl Bereiter, the University of Toronto; Linda Flower, Carnegie-Mellon University; and M. A. K. Halliday, the University of Sydney, for their many writings over the past years. Our thanks to them; we hope that we have not done too great violence to their ideas. Our thanks, also, to the thousands of students whose writing has enraged and cheered us. Special thanks go to Patricia Bandy for typing the four versions of this work so cheerfully and to the staff at Harcourt Brace Jovanovich: Matt Milan, acquisitions editor; Anne Harvey, production editor; Helen Faye, art editor; Bill Shaw, designer; Kim Turner, production manager; and Gene Carter Lettau, our manuscript editor, who really cares about our book.

Contents

HOW TO FIND OUT WHAT YOUR TEACHER EXPECTS AND WANTS

1

Writing successfully in college courses differs from much of the writing you may have done in high school. One of the main differences is that you will be writing papers and essay examinations for many different subjects. We have found that students do better if they know the rules and strategies for writing in various academic subjects, and so we have prepared a book that gives some of the strategies that we think will help to ensure your success. Probably you know many of these strategies already, but reviewing them from time to time will help you sharpen your writing skills and, we think, make the path to success a little bit easier.

And so we are going to give you these strategies specifically for academic writing so that you will be able to write successfully in various educational situations. We won't show you how to write successful love letters or how to fill out application forms better than anyone else or how to write books or poems or other kinds of writing that exist in the world.

Let us begin with a few general strategies which probably do not need much discussion.

> Make sure the papers you hand in are neat. Teachers tend to lower grades on papers that are not typed, are messy, have poor margins, or are generally unattractive. If you are assigned a paper or a report that you can do out of class, you should type it — double-spaced on nonerasable paper. Try to keep good margins and try to avoid strikeovers or messy erasures. If you are writing in class or in an examination, make sure your paper is legible. You may want to skip lines so that you can revise neatly and so your professor will have space to insert comments and corrections. If a teacher can't read your paper, your good ideas will go to waste.

> Get to know your teachers. Teachers remember and often reward students who participate. Teachers appreciate students who ask questions, and most want students to know what kind of writing academic readers prefer. So feel free to raise your hand in class or to talk with your teachers after class or during office hours to find out exactly what their writing standards are. For example, some teachers want you to refer to yourself in your writing; others will mark you down for it.

> Teachers also need and want feedback about their teaching and their materials, so be sure to tell teachers if you like their courses or if you have suggestions for improvement.

> If you have a choice of topics and you can handle any one equally well, choose the one you think the fewest other students will write on. Your teacher

will appreciate a lively change and will read your paper with enthusiasm — which will effect your grade positively.

Remember that the topic that looks simplest often has a trap; a simple statement like "Discuss the causes of World War I" may hide the teacher's desire for an economic interpretation, not a summary.

Remember that some teachers are mainly interested in what you have to say, some are interested in the organization and wording you choose, but almost all are put off by poor punctuation and spelling.

Remember that written language is different from spoken language; reading requires that your audience use different skills than if they were listening.

From your point of view, too, writing requires you to use different skills than talking does. You are going to be writing for a number of people: yourself, other students, and most particularly, teachers. In most cases, you will not be there in person to explain to your readers what you mean or to keep up their interest. Even when you are writing for yourself or taking lecture or reading notes, you will not always remember what was said or written in the text. Therefore, you will have to transform these notes so they will be clear when you reread them at the end of the semester. The reader — even if it is you — has to get most of the information from the typed or written page. As a writer you can never and need not convey all the information you have, but at the same time you should not assume that your reader shares all your experiences. If you write about a trip, you won't include every detail, and yet you cannot expect that your reader has taken the same trip. You have to decide how much you need to include in the text and how much you can expect the reader to fill in.

In the same way you have to judge how much of your personality to include. At times, of course, you will write about yourself, your own experiences, or opinion. Even so,

3

you will recognize that an *informal* style is not the same as conversation. If you read a novel in which the dialogue appears "natural," remember that the author has not transcribed speech with all the *uh's* and stops and starts, but has carefully *written* language that *resembles* speech in some ways. But it is meant to be read, not heard.

People talking together have several advantages over people writing. The main advantage is that they are together — if something is unclear, the listener can say, "What do you mean?" And if the listener understands, the speaker can usually tell from the expression on the listener's face. But the writer cannot tell when the reader misunderstands, so the writer has to use many devices to ensure that the reader understands. We will explore many of these devices in this book.

Writing, however, has some great advantages over speaking: Writing is easier to save and to go back to frequently. You can think of your lecture and reading notes as your own personal written records. They supplement and complement your textbooks. (Although tape recordings — "frozen speech" — can serve you as helpful learning tools, they are less convenient than books and notes, because you need a machine to play tapes back, they are more difficult to scan for the main point, they require more time for listening than does a text for reading the same material, and they don't provide the advantage of condensed notes when you need quick recall of information.) Written documents give people a sense of the permanence of information. For example, a common close to a business telephone call is "I'll send you written confirmation."

Among the many things we think you should know about writing in college are the following six points:

1. Generally both writer and reader think of writing in terms of complete segments and not individual words, phrases, or sentences. Readers read a chap-

ter or an article. Writers write a paragraph or two, a paper, or an essay. Although the individual parts are important, of course, people compose or read the whole. We, too, will spend more time discussing complete segments than smaller parts.

2. Sometimes you know exactly to whom you are writing; more often than not, however, your audience is a *category* of people — teachers, other students, librarians, experts, politicians, or editors of newspapers. In these cases you are writing for — and not to — your audience. Even if you are writing a letter to the manager of a television station protesting the cancellation of a favorite program, you probably will not know the manager personally. Although you may know a lot about television, you won't know the manager's likes and dislikes or programming philosophy. So you will have to assume certain things and write for a hypothetical television station manager.

   In academic writing, your audience will usually be the teacher or a grader who knows more about the topic than you do — but does not know how you are going to approach and shape the information. The writing you may do in many academic situations is often directed at undefined audiences like the hypothetical television station manager, so you should assume that your reader has no more than a general knowledge of what you are writing about. It is usually better to overexplain than not to explain enough.

3. Actually the last sentence applies to most academic writing you do because you are demonstrating to your reader what you know about the subject, how you think, how much effort you have put into learning about your subject and presenting it, how mature you are, or how original you are, or all of these.

In this case you are not informing a poorly defined audience or readers who are ignorant about the subject. Your readers either are trying to help you improve, or they want to evaluate your standing compared to other students or to an ideal paper. So you should think of your academic readers as judges of the quality of your knowledge, thinking, and writing. Like most general readers, your academic readers will cooperate with you by making every effort to understand and to interpret positively what you write. But the main function of your academic readers — teachers and graders — is to act as critics. In this role, academic readers look at your use of language at a literal level; they seek out logical gaps and errors; they notice phrasing, spelling, and punctuation errors; and they relentlessly point out your failures.

4. More often than not, your academic writing shows what you know about a subject and particularly what you think about that subject. To convince your readers, you must make clear how you reach your conclusions and on what evidence you base them. As you write, make sure that the connections between evidence and conclusions will be absolutely clear to your readers; show your reasoning.

5. As a student you will write for several reasons — to remember or record information, to organize or reorganize information, or to interpret or create new information. (When we talk about information, we mean facts, ideas, feelings, and/or attitudes.) In order to accomplish these goals successfully, you will have to master several kinds of writing (see Table 1-1). This table shows that academic writing consists of the three cognitive or thinking processes we have mentioned. It also consists of four major functions: to learn, to convey, to inform, and to

Table 1-1

GENERAL MODEL OF WRITTEN DISCOURSE

Dominant Intention/ Purpose	Primary Audience	Reproduce — Facts	Reproduce — Ideas	Organize/Reorganize — Events	Organize/Reorganize — Visual images, facts, mental states, ideas	Invent/Generate — Ideas, mental states, alternative worlds
						comments on book margins
To learn (metalingual)	Self	copying, taking dictation		retell a story (heard or read)	note, resume, summary, outline, paraphrasing	metaphors analogies
To convey emotions, feelings (emotive)	Self, Others	stream of consciousness		personal story	personal diary, personal letter / portrayal	reflective writing: personal essays
To inform (referential)	Others	quote	fill in a form	narrative report, news, instruction, telegram, announcement, circular	directions, description, technical description, biography, science report/experiment	expository writing definition academic essay/article book review commentary
To convince/ persuade (conative)	Others	citation from authority/expert		letter of application — statement of personal views, opinions	advertisement, letter of advice	argumentative/ persuasive writing: editorial critical essay/ article
To entertain, delight, please (poetic)	Others	quote poetry and prose		given an ending— create a story, create an ending, retell a story	word portrait or sketch	entertainment writing: parody, rhymes
To keep in touch (phatic)	Others	greeting card		postcard	personal letter	humorous greeting

The traditional literary genres and modes can be placed under one or more of these five purposes persuade. You will have to take notes on class lectures and readings, and you will have to reorganize your lecture and reading notes to help you learn. Some teachers may occasionally ask you to present your emotions or feelings about a topic in a personal essay. Most frequently, however, you will have to reorganize or interpret material in order to inform your reader about what you know and what you think. Finally, at times you will have to convince your reader that you understand a book or a set of ideas completely and correctly. Sometimes you will want to let your teacher know that you like an assignment, the course, or the teacher. One student we know always began an examination answer with "This is the most challenging question I have ever had to answer," and ended "I learned a lot doing this assignment." As we indicate in Table 1-1, both are social conventions expressed in writing which tell the reader nothing except how the student feels, and both the reader and the writer know that these sentences are noninformational. They may, however, help the reader to look at the information in the papers more positively and indirectly influence the way the teacher/reader grades such papers.

Whatever the type of writing, each has certain conventions, such as order of information, content stipulations, and stylistic rules established by custom. We normally do not expect a picture postcard to contain an explanation of a mathematics proof. We do expect a recipe to list the ingredients first. Other conventions we all have to observe include spelling, grammar, and punctuation. No matter what field we are in, we all have to learn the conventions of that field. When you receive an assignment, you may need to determine both what sort of thinking it requires and what its main function may be. In the exercise section at the end of this book, we will show you a way to analyze assignments using this grid.

6. Finally, when most people write, they follow a general procedure that includes four main steps: planning, writing, revising, and editing. Although some people are able to combine two or more of these steps, most people need to follow these four steps in that order. *Planning* includes actually deciding what to write about, what information to include, and in what order to present that information. *Writing* includes actually producing a first draft of the finished paper, sometimes putting information in order from beginning to end, and sometimes preparing different parts as you gather the information. *Revising* includes those self-critical steps after the first draft during which the writer changes or reorders ideas. Writers also revise and rewrite following advice and suggestions of other people. *Editing* entails checking the revised paper for punctuation, spelling, readability, and neatness. None of these steps is particularly easy, and none is much fun at times. Nevertheless, most professional writers follow these steps, and we strongly advise you to do so if you wish to succeed.

About the Teacher

Your teachers will help you by giving advice, encouragement, and constructive criticism of your work. You will want to find out from your teachers what they expect from students, what they think the characteristics of good writing are, and what they want you to avoid. Your teachers, however, cannot learn academic writing for you. You have to do the learning yourself — no one can do it for you. Since you are, in the end, the one who is responsible for learning how to write specifically for college, you are the one who has to do it.

You know from experience that you feel good when someone praises your work, says that you have done a good job, and takes an interest in your activities. The same is true of teachers. They also need positive feedback from students in order to feel satisfied and successful. What kinds of feedback do teachers expect? Minimally, they feel good when they see students making an adequate effort to learn. At the next level they feel good when they see students making good progress and learning and when they have a sense that they have contributed to that learning. A third kind of positive feedback for teachers comes from the dialogue they have with students. Asking questions for clarification, praising the teacher for an interesting and useful course — even criticizing the course or method of teaching, provided that you do it constructively and tactfully (giving reasons for your criticism and suggestions for improvements) can all make courses more fruitful for both you and your teacher.

Grading and Marks

About as many grading systems exist as teachers to apply them. Some teachers carefully mark each little error in red; some simply put a letter grade on the top of the paper. We have reviewed some of the research on how teachers mark and on the kinds of comments they make about papers.

Teachers may or may not mark a particular grammatical lapse or spelling mistake; they may or may not use a phrase like *awk* or *stc frg*; they may or may not occasionally write *good* or *interesting* in the margin. Usually, however, they do make some kind of summary comment. We have collected and defined the adjectives they tend to use when they are praising a composition (more often than not they use the opposites of these adjectives), and what they mean by them:

1. An *accurate* essay provides correct information.
2. An *appealing* essay is enjoyable to read, able to evoke a certain atmosphere, and/or appeal to the senses and emotions successfully.
3. An *effective* essay is eloquent, vivid, and emphatic in providing a convincing, arresting argument or description that makes the writer's point.
4. An *original* treatment of the topic is inspired and imaginative, possessing a freshness of feeling. It interests and stimulates the reader.
5. A *concisely* written composition tells the maximum amount in a minimun of words. Its simple, straight-to-the-point style captures the essential ideas efficiently.
6. A composition is well *connected* when there are clear transitions between ideas and sentences. It successfully juxtaposes topics.
7. A composition is well *developed* when it elaborates and explains main ideas thoroughly.
8. A *consistently* written composition has a unity of content and form, mood, style, and ideas throughout.
9. A *focused* composition presents *one* thesis with sufficient elaboration related to that thesis.
10. An essay is *tightly organized* when it has a well-ordered, logical, cohesive, coherent sequence of paragraphs reflecting the writer's clear, unified vis-

ion of the relationships between ideas presented. The writer doesn't digress.

11. A *clearly* written composition is comprehensible, not obscure.

12. A *detailed* treatment of the topic contains many specific examples, each of which is elaborated.

13. An *informative* composition reports many facts about and/or aspects of the topic; it usually gives new information to the reader.

14. In a *penetrating* essay the writer reveals good perception and sensitive ability to explore complex ideas in-depth. The writer often points out several sides to an issue.

15. The writer has been *precise* when he or she defines ideas and terms sharply.

16. An essay contains a *critical* treatment of the subject if the writer has exercised judgement to evaluate good and/or bad aspects of the topic.

17. A composition written in an *honest* manner is unpretentious and matter-of-fact in its treatment of the subject. It expresses true and sincere feelings.

18. In a *humorous* essay the writer succeeds in being witty or in taking a novel approach to the topic.

19. A *personal* composition reveals the writer's impressions, experiences, opinions, and feelings.

20. A composition written in a *sophisticated* manner displays the writer's awareness of complex social and cultural realities.

21. A *fluidly* written essay is graceful, flowing, and articulate.

22. In a *formally* written composition the writer avoids colloquial language and maintains distance from the reader by not being too personal, social, or chatty.

23. An essay is *figurative* if it contains metaphors and images that convey ideas in a colorful way.

24. A composition written in a *lively* way is stimulating and vivacious. It shows the writer's interest in the topic.
25. The language of an essay is *poetic* if it is similar to that used in poetry without seeming artificial or grandiloquent.
26. The essay is *subtle* if the writer suggests ideas or feelings rather than telling them in a literal manner.
27. A composition has adequate *variety* if it doesn't strike the reader as monotonous and avoids too much repetition of words, ideas, and/or sentence structures.

Of course, these definitions we have given do not tell the full story. Sometimes, for example, a teacher might use a word like *penetrating* to refer to content or to a general impression of you as a writer. We also found that some of these adjectives apply to some kinds of academic writing more than to others. So in Table 1-2 we have classified these terms according to whether they apply to specific kinds of writing and to whether the teacher refers to the content of the composition (*what* is said), the form of the composition (*how* it is said), or the effect of the composition (*how* the teacher *feels* about the content or style).

When you read an instructor's comment, this chart can help you understand the general emphasis of the comment and more specifically, it can help you clarify your questions to the instructor when you go in for a conference. You might ask something like, "When you said the paper was not original, did you mean that the content was too familiar or that the whole thing struck you as trite?" If you get the answer to that question, maybe you will have some information with which to make the next essay better.

Table 1-2   CRITERIA TO BE SELECTED

DOMINANT PURPOSE	Representative tasks	Content	Form	Effect
Metalingual	copy, note, resume, summary, paraphrase, outline	focused, concise	connected, developed, consistent focused, tightly organized	serious
Emotive	personal story, personal essay, portrayal, diary	critical, personal, sophisticated	subtle, fluid	honest, humorous, personal, appealing
Referential	narrative report, description, expository composition, academic essay, directions	clear, detailed, informative, penetrating, precise, original, accurate	detailed, precise, tightly organized, focused, developed connected	penetrating, serious, effective
Conative	letter of application, statement of opinion, argumentative or persuasive composition, editorial	original, penetrating, subtle	effective, consistent, tightly organized, focused	appealing, original, convincing
Poetic	story, poem, play	subtle, concise, original	fluid, formal, figurative, poetic, varied	lively, appealing
Phatic	postcard, personal letter	personal	formal	lively, appealing, honest, humorous

HOW TO WRITE IN
COLLEGE—AN OVERVIEW

2

In this brief chapter we would like to present you with some general advice on two topics related to most academic assignments. The first topic concerns an overall strategy for tackling any assignment, whether it be attending a lecture, reading a book, or writing a paper. The second topic deals with some general principles of discourse—what you hear, read, say, or write—and particularly how such discourse is usually organized. We urge you to memorize Figure 2-1 (p. 18) and Table 2-1 (p. 19) and to use them; the more you participate in academic work, the more you will be able to define and control it. You should not simply be a passive recipient: Take charge of your learning. Make it yours. Look for cues, and test your own hypotheses about each subject.

A Strategy for Learning

When you go to a lecture or other class, approach a text-book or other assigned reading, or write a paper, you can follow some *general* strategies to help you make your mind more productive. At the same time, remember that each subject you study has *specific* strategies, some of which we will cover later.

1. In each course make sure that you know *what* you are supposed to do, to remember, to learn, or to write. You should determine the teacher's specific instructions or objectives (which are usually given at the beginning of the course). If the instructor is not clear enough, you should ask. In reading or listening, are you to get a general sense of what is being presented or are you to focus on details and procedures? In writing are you to give back infor-mation, reorganize it, or interpret it? Do not assume that all teachers want the same thing. Some want facts and generalizations, as many as possible; some want a lot of organization and argument.

2. Determine what level of difficulty you will face, by asking yourself questions like the following: "Can I do this? How is this assignment difficult for me? How will I do it? What will I need to take into account? What preparation should I have? Why should I study or take notes on this?" These ques-tions help get your mind set. When you go to a class, they help you determine whether you should work through the problems and issues the teacher dis-cusses or whether you should treat the information you receive in class as background material. When you read, you need to answer these questions to decide whether you should skim and take general notes or whether you have to trudge through the

work page by page and take detailed notes. When you write, you have to decide how much additional information you need to acquire. In part, the kind of material will give you a clue as will the length of the assignment. But short assignments, in terms of numbers of pages may take as much time as long ones, depending on what the task requires.

3. Determine what sequence you should follow. The sequence will come in part from the answers to the questions listed in 2. Also, try to note when you need help and when you are progressing smoothly. Pause briefly to ask yourself, "Am I getting it? Does it make sense?" If not, ask the teacher or, if you are reading or writing, go back to where you began to lose control of your material.

4. Check your understanding after you are through. What questions remain for you? Did you find the listening, reading, or writing easy or hard? Did you use the best procedure? Did you follow the whole sequence of activities?

After practicing with these questions on several assignments, you will find they become automatic. Figure 2-1 summarizes them.

Plans and Structures in Discourse

One of the ways you can help yourself answer the questions in the first part of this chapter is by determining the structure of the various kinds of discourse you will read, write, speak, and listen to. In most societies these different kinds of discourse are organized according to one or more limited sets of principles called *structures*.

A good speaker or writer knows how a specific kind of discourse should be organized and presents the material

Figure 2-1

CHECKLIST OF LEARNING STRATEGIES WITH
PARTICULAR REFERENCE TO COMPOSITION

A. Do I know what I am supposed to do?
   1. Are the instructions clear? Do I understand them?
   2. Am I sure of the teacher's objectives? Are these defensible alternatives?
B. Can I do the task?
   1. Do I see its importance?
   2. How is it difficult for me?
   3. Have I a plan?
   4. Have I made all the necessary preparations?
C. Do I know all the steps?
   1. Have I checked my progress?
   2. Do I need more help?
D. Have I done what I was supposed to do?
   1. Did I include everything that is relevant?
   2. Have I made the necessary revisions?
   3. Was any part hard for me? Which part and why?
   4. Did the procedure work? What am I good at and what are my weak spots?

using that organization almost automatically. A good listener or reader picks up that structure just as automatically. Most people know a fairy or folk tale is coming as soon as they hear the phrase "Once upon a time. . . ." They know that the organization of what will follow will have a temporal sequence: First things will come first, and the order of the segments of writing or talking will follow a time sequence. Such structure is sometimes referred to as a schema or frame. In many cases what you will hear or read will follow the narrative or story structure which is the most common structure. But much talking and writing in academic courses have other types of organization. Table 2-1 outlines the basic kinds of organization that most people use for the purposes we set forth in Table 1-1. This table is one of the most

TYPICAL ORGANIZATIONS
Table 2-1 OF DISCOURSE

ORGANIZED BY TIME

Narration: Chronological development. May be rearranged with flashbacks or may have two or more simultaneous series of events.

Process: Chronological or step–by–step development. May include a list of parts or ingredients.

Typical signals:

once	first	second	later	and
next	after	before	then	

Cause–effect: Like process but may go from effect to cause or cause to effect.

Typical signals:

the reason for	consequently	therefore	by means of	thus
result from	and so	because	effect	

ORGANIZED BY SPACE

Description: Develops by a geometrical or geographical arrangement—usually horizontal, vertical, or circular. May follow a map or a topographical arrangement.

Typical signals:

besides	below	down from	as we move	around
above	in front of	near	as you go	about
next to	behind	following	proceeding	

ORGANIZED BY COMMON LOGIC

Classification: Develops by dividing objects or events into parts and explaining relationships or differences between parts.

Definition: Develops by giving distinctions of the object or event from others similar to it.

Typical signals:

to constitute	to limit to	let us define	may be divided
progressive	succession	as follows	into
is called	is seen as	(a), (b), (c)	is made up of
: (colon)			(1), (2), (3)

Comparison–contrast: Organized by relating or differentiating two or more objects or events.

Typical signals:

may be distinguished from	as
differs from	on the other hand
compared to	but
distinct from	

important in the book, because it shows you how to make sense of what you hear and read and shows you the major ways to organize whatever you write — even your own notes.

Essentially, there are seven kinds of structures. Each of the seven is almost automatic for the experienced reader or writer. Each provides a formula for writers and speakers to use when presenting information or ideas to most readers and listeners. Good writers and speakers signal the appropriate structure clearly. We shall be referring to Table 2-1 frequently throughout the rest of the book; if you learn the content of the table well, you will be able to write, speak, read, and listen more effectively. The seven typical structures are like a common code for most academic discourse.

To help you see these categories at work, we have taken some paragraphs from the biography, *Charles Carroll of Carrollton*. We have indicated in the headings how we would classify the dominant purpose of the paragraphs. See if you can recognize the clues that led us to our decision.

Narration
On July 2, 1773, the Lower House unanimously declared the governor's proclamation illegal. Then they [the members of the assembly] adjourned and in a body marched through the streets of the capital — with most of the townspeople following after — to the Carroll House on Spa Creek, where they thanked the First Citizen in person. He accepted their speeches as gracefully as if he had been a public character all his life. In fact, he was so calm and self-contained that he rather disappointed his audience (p. 114).

Process
The American colonies could not afford to spare either the troops or the money for a military expedition into Canada, but now that the first amateurish attempts at diplomacy had failed General Washington succeeded in convincing Congress that it was the only thing to try. He shared the prevalent American belief that Canadian help was absolutely necessary to the success of the rebellion against England, and felt sure that an armed force sent not to oppress but to liberate and incidentally conciliate the Canadians

would immediately encourage them to rebel too against the mother country. All America joined him in thinking that Canada really longed to rebel, but simply lacked the moral courage. Washington and America were later proved to have been mistaken — but this was only September 1775. For a while the Canadian campaign went well enough: General Richard Montgomery captured Montreal and there was great hope that General Benedict Arnold would be as successful at Quebec. Instead, Arnold was defeated and severely wounded and Montgomery, one of the most brilliantly capable American officers, was killed. Not only had the attack upon Quebec failed; there was little prospect of facility to make another attempt (pp. 134–35).

Cause-Effect

Thus when the Attorney-General died, the following year, it was eighteen-year-old Charles who took over the family burdens. His younger brother, Daniel, was able to stay in Europe and complete his education, but Charles, the student of the two, had to leave school when he had no more than finished his philosophy. All his life he was bitter about the frustration of his plan to study law. He wrote many years later: "I have from the time I came from school, in the year 1720, to the year 1757, been a constant servant of my family" (p. 22).

Description

He had been thoroughly educated in the family tradition, had Charles Carroll of Carrollton. His opinion of the English government was, even more than he himself realized, as hereditary as his high-bridged nose. He was a born fighter, a born crusader, a born rebel — in a word, he was an Irishman. Hatred of political England had been bred into him. He had hated it consciously ever since his father, that day eight years before in Paris, had summed up the family history and the family situation. Ever since then he had wanted passionately to be, some day, free of the oppression which English rule had meant to his people. He saw the Stamp Act controversy, clear-eyed, as an opening wedge (p. 78).

Classification

Another group of people translated the Stamp Act into terms of money instead of infringed liberty, and amounted to a great deal more. These were the people upon whose businesses the tax would actually impose more or less financial hardship — the lawyers, the merchants, and the owners and editors of newspapers. With one eye on posterity, they spoke, like the idealists, in capitals. Unlike the idealists, they were not sincere in doing so, for most of them cared very little for the beautiful abstractions of liberty. They were interested in money, and they rebelled at the idea of being taxed from two sources instead of one; the colonial assemblies, they considered, were bad enough without adding to them the Crown. The lawyers were afraid that a tax on legal documents would take the joy out of the great eighteenth-century recreation of going to court about little or nothing. The editors, much poorer than the lawyers as a class, dreaded a tax which would hit them two ways, since it affected advertisements as well as newspaper. The merchants resented any move to regulate the customs — by the use of stamped paper or otherwise — for many of them had been successfully smuggling their goods in for years. One historian declares that nine-tenths of the American merchants were smugglers, and he includes among the gentlemen mixed up in the smuggling trade such luminaries as Alexander Hamilton, Jonathan Trumbull, and John Hancock (p. 76).

Definition
Tea was the only commodity mentioned in the late unlamented Townshend Acts on which the impost duty had been retained. Patriots in the various colonies were still bound by the non-importation agreements which they had signed several years before, so by common consent the business of importing tea became recognized as a nefarious one. According to law it might not be imported by the British colonies from any country except England; and the colonies had no idea of paying the English threepence tax. The most high-minded patriots favored doing without tea altogether; but others enjoyed killing two birds with one stone by not only boycotting the British but smuggling into America tea bought from the Dutch or other competitors of the British. Needless to say it was the latter idea which took hold, and tea smuggling became a recognized and profitable business (p. 17).

Comparison-Contrast
Unlike the Stamp Act, this measure could not be objected to on the grounds that the British ministry had no right to impose it. It was not an internal tax but an external one. But even so the ministry had anticipated protests, and had tried to soften it by

guaranteeing that the money which it proposed to raise would not be used anywhere except in America. That is, while the tax would take money from the American colonies, it would do so for the purpose of giving it right back to them (p. 92).

Ellen Hart Smith, Charles Carroll of Carrollton. Cambridge, Mass.: Harvard University Press, 1942.

In most cases the writer, Smith, signals the organization in the first sentence of the paragraph. As you practice your own reading and writing see how quickly you can spot these signals. Also see if you can make your paragraphs — in fact your whole composition — clearer to your readers by signaling the structure you are using. You should note, of course, that the book from which we took the examples is a biography, a narrative by definition. But embedded within any narrative, as in our example, will be other types of organization. In your own writing you will also have a major structure for the whole composition, and you will use different paragraph structures to support that organization.

HOW TO TAKE NOTES IN LECTURES AND FROM BOOKS—WRITING TO REMEMBER

3

You will probably do more writing for yourself than for anyone else while you are in school. You will take notes from a teacher or from a film, tape, or video demonstration; you will outline the main point of a chapter in a textbook or a library book; you will take notes from a computer lesson; you will take field or laboratory notes; or you will write up the highlights of an interview. At times you may hand in to a teacher what you wrote or share it with a friend or use it for a class discussion, but usually the person who will be using your writing is you—either as you study or as you prepare a paper. In this chapter, we will show you what various kinds of research and many people's experience say about ways of making your writing to remember more effective.

Listening and Writing

Writing to Remember What You Hear —
Helping Yourself

You will be doing a fair amount of listening during classes, and very often you will be asked to recall what you heard for an examination or a paper. As we showed in Chapter 1, oral language differs from written language in a number of ways. When you write down lecture or other class notes, don't think of yourself as taking dictation, but as trying to capture in visible form what you have heard. The following is an excerpt from a college lecture on contemporary culture; the lecturer is talking informally from memory rather than from a set of detailed notes (there is a misstatement in the lecture):

We happen to be in a society which is divided on ethnic grounds, economic grounds and also quite divided on the nature of the culture. About 20 years ago Dwight McDonald wrote a book in which he said there were three main cultures in the United States, what he called mass-cult, mid-cult and hi-cult. He was applying this in terms of the adult population but the same thing certainly holds true for the child population. If one can make gross distinctions in, let's say, types of reading, a mass-cult person would read romances, possibly a man would read the works of Louis L'Amour. Anybody not know who Louis L'Amour is? He is one of the most successful living authors in this country and he writes Westerns. He has written something like 200 of them. He does very well. They all follow very much the same plot.

A mid-cult person might well read things that are hopefully among the 12 Literary Guild selections. They might not read them but they would join. A lot of people join Book-of-the-Month Club without reading the books. Then in terms of magazines the mass-cult person might read *True*. The mid-cult person might read *Esquire*.

And then there is a very small group which McDonald called hi-cult. Which is to say a group of people generally found in large urban communities like New York and San Francisco and Chicago. If they belong to any book club they might go on to Reader's Subscription. They tend to read not the best seller but the more avantgarde novel.

There are three, in a sense, sets of tastes. Now across these tastes, however, tend to be certain things which transcend or cut across these obviously broad categories. One of the interesting phenomena in the publishing world is the advent of marketing specialists so that a novel, for instance, that appeared recently, or three or four years ago . . . John Irving's *The World According to Garp* . . . have any of you read it? or heard of it? You will. This was a hi-cult book. It started out as a hi-cult book. They thought it would sell reasonably well but then got picked up by one of the book clubs, I think Book-of-the-Month Club and moved into, in a sense, the mid-cult world. Now its paperback publisher is publishing it in five different dust jackets with an estimated publication of something like five or six million, a high media hype and intends to get this book into as many households as possible, but it would be better now to get into some other questions, at least in terms of details. This is one book that moved from one culture to a broader one. Student: What was the name of the book again?

The World According to Garp. GARP. It has ideas and sex so that you'll probably feel fairly — uh — gory, I suspect, and also it will eventually become a film. They usually don't promote something that heavily unless it is to become one.

On the other hand, there are certain things that have started out to a certain extent as mass-cult phenomena and then were quickly absorbed by the hi-cult world. One of these was Peanuts, to a certain extent. It's now everybody's. But how many of you remember Pogo? Pogo in a sense simply started out as a daily strip but then as it increasingly became the property of fewer and fewer people, very special concerned groups of people came to read it. I think the reverse is true of Doonesbury. It started out particularly for the radical student audience, well-educated, but it has become increasingly popular. So things do move back and forth across these cultural bounds. They are not, as I indicate, clear cut. Two phenomena I will come to later have tended possibly to shift some of these hard and fast boundary things.

As we said, the lecture is not particularly well-organized or accurate, but it is typical of many academic lectures. How much should you write down and what kind of notes should you take? There is a fair amount of information in this segment — which probably lasted five minutes of a class, but only some of the information is worth remembering. The teacher starts off with a main point — about three types of culture — supports the point with examples, and then shows that the three types are not hard-and-fast categories. As a student in the class, you would not have a transcript, but would be catching all of this on the fly. What should you take down?

Look for the main points or the generalization. Since the lecture topic in the course outline was *Popular Literature*; you might then guess that the lecturer is probably going to spend part of the time defining popular literature and giving examples. The lecturer might also classify types of popular literature. The structure may well be logical, not narrative or descriptive. The lecturer might also explain why the literature is popular. As you look at this segment, you will notice that the lecturer begins with the word *divided*, and proceeds to suggest ways of division and then the three divisions. The word should tip you off that some sort of classification or division will follow. The lecturer also repeats the word *three*, so that you can guess that there will be three subdivisions. In the midst of these subdivisions are a number of examples; you probably do not need to write down the examples unless they help you remember. The examples in this lecture are by way of illustration, but notice that one student asked for the spelling of the name. If the student needs the correct spelling just for a lecture note, the information is probably not too useful, although some people remember by example. In addition to the three divisions, you should include in your notes the fact that some books cross divisions and that the divisions are flexible. Again, you might want to include an example, both the one the lecturer gives and your own. Adding your own will help fix the ideas in your mind.

Some good students begin taking class notes by jotting down the main ideas of the lecture (Box 3-1). As soon after class as possible they look over their jottings and add other examples that occur to them, questions they may want to ask, and comments they may have on the content of the lecture. Sometimes, they might ask the teacher to clarify any points they have not completely understood.

Box 3-1

---

3 LEVELS CULTURE IN U.S.
Mass — Westerns. what about spies and detectives?
Mid — Book of Month, Esquire, Women's example?
High — Reader's Subscription, special groups like horses? history?
(Ask whether categories make sense.)

Other successful students take the rough notes and that evening or as soon as possible summarize and reorganize the notes into a more permanent form (Box 3-2).

In both cases the students have not simply taken down the words idly, but have done some thinking about and reorganizing of the material. The strategy is effective, because very often a person taking on-the-spot notes will not remember even a week later why a phrase was important. The lecture has slipped out of the memory and the words are not enough to jog it. In fact, the weak listener puts down words (usually nouns) not phrases, and words are harder to remember than phrases.

When you take listening notes, then, look for structuring signals, take down phrases, check examples, and add your own. Most important, look over your notes that day, and either rewrite them or add information and questions to make sure they are clear to you.

Box 3-2

Rough Notes
  Society divided on culture
      mass-cult, mid-cult, high-cult
      adults and children
  mass cult — romances, westerns, Lamour
  mid-cult — literary guild, Book of Month
  Hi-cult — N.Y., S.F.
  Culture is taste, books go across culture
  Marketing: World Acc. to Garp, Peanuts start high go mass, Pogo
      other way, Doonesbury

Copied Notes
  Society divided into levels of culture and reading
      Mass-cult — romances, westerns, Harlequin, soaps
      Mid-cult — Book of Month, PBS
      Hi-cult — classics? avant-garde
  These levels a matter of taste, but some works marketed to sell to
  several groups. *World According to Garp, Peanuts,* M*A*S*H*?
      Some books become more and more specialized to one group.
  Pogo, Paper Chase

Controlling Your Lectures

You should also become aware of the differences between lecturers. The professor talking about contemporary culture has one or two main points and uses a lot of examples. The lecture is organized but loose. On the other hand, some lecturers write out what they have to say and read it, especially when they are working through a complex argument or summarizing a lot of research. Their lectures will be dense and packed with information. As a result, you will have difficulty taking notes, but fortunately in most courses, the lecturer starts off slowly and picks up speed. You will pick up speed, too. But you can help the teacher help you. Don't be afraid to ask questions like: "So what you are saying is ... ?" "Could you briefly summarize your point?" "Could you give us another example?" "Do you mean that ... ?"

Reading and Writing

Taking Reading Notes

During your academic career, in addition to taking notes on what you hear in classes, you will take notes on your reading. Much of the reading will be in textbooks that you own and can refer to, but you will find it useful to take notes on the books you own because note taking helps you learn and remember. A great deal of reading, however, will be in library books and journal articles. At times, when you are working on a term paper, you will have to provide exact quotations and references. Most often, though, you will need to read a book or an article and remember the main points of what you have read. In literature courses you will be asked to read novels or plays and remember characters and scenes or major ideas and themes. Some people use expensive guides that do the note taking for you, but in many cases such luxuries will not be available, and you will have to do the reading and the note taking for yourself.

After interviewing a number of successful students and looking at the textbooks they have used and the notes they have taken, we can offer you some suggestions:

Do not merely use a "hi-liner" or underline or make vertical lines in the margin unless you have a system, or you may not remember why you marked what you did. And some textbooks are so compact, particularly mathematics or science texts, that you may be tempted to underline almost every sentence. In other texts, underlining helps you read more slowly and look for the main points. Skim the assignment once before you underline.

You may want to write guide notes or comments in the margin of a textbook and make an index for yourself on the inside cover.

If the textbook is in mathematics or one of the sciences, you can help yourself if you draw diagrams, write out key formulas in the margins, or work out the sample problems in the margin. In the example in Figure 3-1, underlining will not help you remember as much as a marginal diagram will.

Most successful students take reading notes, using either a notebook or a set of index cards. The reading notes consist of the main point of the book or article and the major supporting ideas of examples. As in taking lecture notes, the successful students note the organization of the piece of writing. They also include significant details that help them remember what they have read or the kinds of details that they suspect will occur on examinations.

Box 3-3 (pp. 33-4) shows history text that belonged to two students. One student underlined with the heavy lines, another with the spidery lines. We find it hard to determine the reasons for each reader's choices or whether one reader made better selections than the other.

If you were to take reading notes, they might look like this:

QUASI WAR WITH FRANCE

After 1796, U.S. relations with France got worse. France thought it could use some rights of seizing ships as G.B. and get at Adams. Adams's advisers divided; A. wanted peace, sent 3 men to negotiate. Talleyrand (Fr.) wanted a loan and bribes. Americans said no, reported to Adams who gave report of "XYZ Affair" which told of bribe. This aroused U.S. spirit.

The notes follow a chronological order as signalled by the writers' use of *as, therefore, where, then*, and other time-signaling words. They form a summary of the passage rather than a series of notes, which might not be in sentence form.

Figure 3-1

Example of Student Interaction with a Text: Transforming an Equation into a Diagram

By calculations similar to those on pages 139 and 140, you can show that this equation is equivalent to the equation

$$\frac{x^2}{a^2} - \frac{y^2}{b^2} = 1, \qquad (1)$$

where

$$b^2 = c^2 - a^2 > 0 \text{ and } b > 0.$$

As with the corresponding equation of an ellipse (page 140), the steps are reversible, and accordingly a point $U(x, y)$ is on $\mathcal{H}$ if and only if its coordinates satisfy Equation (1).

Similarly, a hyperbola with center at the origin, foci $F_1(0, c)$ and $F_2(0, -c)$, and absolute value of the difference of the distances equal to $2a$, $0 < a < c$, has Cartesian equation.

$$\frac{y^2}{a^2} - \frac{x^2}{b^2} = 1. \qquad (2)$$

The value of the constant a in Equations (1) and (2) might be greater than, equal to, or less than the value of b.

A hyperbola $\mathcal{H}$ with an equation of the form (1) or (2) is symmetric with respect to both coordinate axes. Thus if $S(x, y)$ is a point of $\mathcal{H}$, then so are $S'(x, -y)$, $S''(-x, y)$, and $S'''(-x, -y)$.

If you replace y with 0 in Equation (1), you obtain $\frac{x^2}{a^2} = 1$, or $x = \pm a$. Thus a and $-a$ are the x-intercepts of a hyperbola of the form (1). If you replace x with 0 in Equation (1), you obtain $\frac{y^2}{b^2} = -1$. Since $\frac{y^2}{b^2}$ is always nonnegative, the hyperbola has no y-intercepts.

In a similar manner, you can show that a hyperbola with an equation of the form (2) has y-intercepts a and $-a$ and no x-intercepts.

Wooten, William, Edwin F. Beckenbach, Frank J. Fleming, *Modern Analytic Geometry*. Boston: Houghton Mifflin, 1975, pp. 146–147. Reprinted by permission of the publishers.

Box 3-3

stead of Adams. The result was a near disaster for the Federalists. They elected a majority of their presidential electors, despite the electioneering tactics of the French government, whose efforts may have boomeranged and helped the Federalists. But when the electors balloted in the various states, some of the Pinckney men declined to vote for Adams, and a still larger number of the Adams men declined to vote for Pinckney. So Pinckney received fewer votes than Jefferson, and Adams only three more than Jefferson. The new president was to be a Federalist, but the vice president was to be a Republican!

By virtue of his diplomatic services during the Revolution, his writings as a conservative political philosopher, and his devotion to the public weal as he saw it, "Honest John" Adams ranks as one of the greatest American statesmen. Like most prominent members of the illustrious Adams family afterward, however, he lacked the politician's touch which is essential for successful leadership in a republic society. Even Washington, remote and austere as he sometimes seems to have been, was fairly adept at conciliating factions and maintaining party harmony. Unwisely, the new president

chose to continue Washington's department heads in office. Most of them were friends of Hamilton, and they looked to him for advice, though he held no official post.

QUASI WAR WITH FRANCE

As American relations with Great Britain and Spain improved in consequence of Jay's and Pinckney's treaties, relations with France, now under the government of the Directory, went from bad to worse. Despite the victory of the Federalists in the election of 1796, the leaders of the Directory assumed that France had the sympathy and support of the mass of the American people and could undermine the Adams administration by frustrating it in foreign affairs. Therefore the French, asserting that they were applying the same principles of neutral rights as the United States and Great Britain had adopted in Jay's Treaty, continued to capture American ships on the high seas and, in many cases, to imprison the crews. When Minister Monroe left France after his recall, the French went out of their way to show their affection for him and for the Republican party. When the South Carolina Federalist Charles Cotesworth Pinckney, a brother of Thomas Pinckney,

Box 3-3 (cont. from p. 33)

arrived in France to replace Monroe, the Directory considered him *persona non grata* and refused to receive him as the official representative of the United States.

War seemed likely unless the Adams administration could settle the difficulties with France. Some of the president's advisers, in particular his secretary of state, the stiff-backed New England Francophobe Timothy Pickering favored war. Others urged a special effort for peace, and even Hamilton approved the idea of appointing commissioners to approach the Directory. Adams, himself a peace man, appointed a bipartisan commission of three: C. C. Pinckney, the recently rejected minister; John Marshall, a Virginia Federalist, afterward famous as the great chief justice of the United States; and Elbridge Gerry, a Massachusetts Republican but a personal friend of the president's. In France, in 1797, the three Americans were met by three agents of the Directory's foreign minister, Prince Talleyrand, who had a reputation as the wizard of European diplomacy but who did not understand the psychology of Americans, even though he had lived for a time in the United States. Talleyrand's agents demanded a loan for France and a bribe for French officials before they would deal with Adams's commissioners. The response of the commissioners was summed up in Pinckney's laconic words: "No! No! Not a sixpence!"

When Adams received the commissioners' report, he sent a message to Congress in which he urged readiness for war, denounced the French for their insulting treatment of the United States, and vowed he would not appoint another minister to France, until he knew the minister would be "received, respected and honored as the representative of a great, free, powerful and independent nation." The Republicans, doubting the president's charge that the United States had been insulted, asked for proof. Adams then turned the commissioners' report over to Congress, after deleting the names of the three Frenchmen and designating them only as Messrs. X., Y., and Z. When the report was published, the "XYZ Affair" provoked an even greater reaction than Adams had bargained for. It aroused the martial spirit of most Americans, made the Federalists more

Richard N. Current, T. Harry Williams, Frank Friedel, *American History: A Survey*, Fifth Edn., New York (Knopf), Vol. 1, 1979, p. 45.

When people look for the main idea in an argumentative book or article (or the theme in a literary work), they adopt one of the following strategies — not all of them work for each text read — but one of them probably will.

Check the title for key words. (Why is the passage called "Quasi War with France"?)

Look for repetitions. What is repeated is often important (Federalist and Republican).

Look for contrasts and oppositions. Many writers set up their ideas through contrast. (Are Federalist and Republican contrasted? How?)

Look for parallels and comparisons. (How are the British and French compared?)

If the book is a novel, check what the narrator comments. (Those comments may be the author's or reflect the author's in some way.)

Look at the beginning and the ending. (Openings and closings often contain the major ideas in summary form.)

Look at the organization; it can tip you off to the main idea. (Remember Table 1 in Chapter 2.)

Look for words that show the author's bias. ("Stiff-backed ... Francophobe" describes Pickering. Why don't the authors like him?)

Summarizing and Outlining

One problem the students who marked the history text seemed to have was determining the main idea of the section. In the note form we suggested — a summary of the "quasi war passage" — we kept the authors' title. That helped us focus on how close to war the Americans and French came and on how much it was like a real war. Writing a summary means going for the main ideas of a passage or book. When you look for the main idea, you

should beware of letting interesting details—names and
odd facts—keep you from the central idea.

Remember *The Wizard of Oz?* Would the following
summary give you an idea of the film?

> Dorothy and her dog Toto are caught in a cyclone and
> the picture changes from black and white to color. In
> her adventures she sees all her friends and enemies
> from her real life changed into a scarecrow, a tinman,
> a lion, a witch, and a wizard. There are two wicked
> witches and one good one. Dorothy destroys both the
> wicked ones. She finally returns home.

There is nothing wrong in this summary, but it leaves out
the journey, the needs of the companions, and the way by
which Dorothy returns. The writer of this summary was
caught by details but somehow did not put them in the
proper order of importance.

Summaries are not easy to write, but they are useful,
particularly if you are faced with reading many articles or
chapters from books. You will need to remember them and
know which ones you want to review for a paper or examination.

One researcher's tips for making summaries include
the following:

1. Delete trivial information and important but redun-
   dant information.
2. Substitute generalizations for specifics.
3. Look for the thesis and topic sentences. If you can't
   find them, write them yourself.
4. Combine topic sentences *across* paragraphs.

Outlining as Note Taking

In addition to producing a summary, you will find it
useful to produce an outline of what you have read or

heard. An outline condenses the original in a different way; it gives not only the main ideas but the organization of the text or lecture. To produce an outline, therefore, you are less concerned with writing a continuous reduction of the text than with showing the main and subordinate ideas in some relationship.

Let us suppose you have been assigned the following article. You go to the library and read it, but you want to remember not only the main ideas, but also the criticisms. An outline might be the best method to follow.

THERMO-PHYSICAL CHARACTERISTICS OF GLACIERS TOWARD A RATIONAL CLASSIFICATION

By Maynard M. Miller

(Department of Geology, Michigan State University, East Lansing, Michigan 48823, U.S.A. and Foundation for Glacier and Environmental Research, Pacific Science Center, Seattle, Washington 98109, U.S.A.)

Abstract

Forty years ago, Ahlmann considered the thermo-physical character of ice masses as a basis for differentiating glaciers into two broad geophysical groups: (1) *polar* and (2) *temperate*. About the same time, Lagally sub-divided glaciers into corresponding thermodynamic categories: (1) *kalt* and (2) *warmen*. By this it was understood that the temperature of a polar, or "cold", glacier was perennially sub-freezing throughout, except for a shallow surface zone which might be warmed for a few centimeters each year by seasonal atmospheric variations. Conversely, in a temperate, or "warm", glacier, the temperature below a recurring winter chill layer was consistently at the pressure melting point. As these terms are thermodynamic in connotation, glaciers of the polar type may exist at relatively low altitudes if their elevations are sufficiently great. Temperate glaciers may be found even above the Arctic Circle at elevations low enough that chilling conditions are not induced by the lapse rate.

In these distinctions, it is implied that regardless of geographical location a glacier's mean internal temperature represents an identifiable characteristic which can be shown critically to affect the mass and liquid balance of ice masses and significantly to relate climatic influences to glacier regimes. The importance of these implications, and the fact that they are based on a gross, sometimes changing, and always difficult to measure, thermophysical characteristic, makes some explicit terminology desirable.

To some extent Ahlmann addressed this problem by introducing a subordinate classification, *sub-polar* glaciers. In these, the penetration of seasonal warmth involved only a shallow surface layer at 0°C, but still to a depth substantially greater than the superficial warming experienced in summer on polar glaciers. Lagally also recognized an intermediate type which he called "transitional", characterized by a relatively deep penetration of 0°C englacial conditions during the summer. These pioneering efforts reflect Ahlmann's experience with glaciers in the high Arctic and Lagally's with the Alpine glaciers of southern Europe. Although some confusion has resulted from alternate application of these different terms, both definitions can be useful. Further to refine the classification, a modified terminology is suggested by the writer. This involves introducing a fourth category, substituting the term *sub-temperate* for Lagally's "transitional" type on the basis that it is etymologically more consistent with the Ahlmann terminology which has remained most commonly in use. Thus, two distinct transitional categories are identified. These categories, sub-polar and sub-temperate, typify ice sheets during changes from fully polar to fully temperate englacial conditions — a situation pertaining during the waning and waxing stages of deglaciation and reglaciation.

A review of the literature reveals further problems. Flint and others have considered geophysically temperate glaciers as most typical of the inland glaciation which covered much of Europe, northern North America and Siberia during the expanded phases of the Pleistocene, whereas others including Ahlmann have suggested that the massive continental glaciers of the Pleistocene were geophysically polar. Thus, the latter advocates consider that present-day Antarctic and Greenland ice sheets represent conditions comparable to those which pertained in the Laurentide and Cordilleran ice sheets. New insights have developed, however, through deep drilling and englacial temperature measurements carried out in a number of different geographical locations in recent years. Such research has shown that each of the geophysical categories can pertain in a glacier system if there is sufficient range of latitude, area and elevation for the requisite climatological factors to pertain.

Because of the foregoing considerations, it is probable that *polar, sub-polar, sub-temperate* and *temperate* thermal conditions coexisted in different parts of continental glaciers during the Pleistocene maxima. At times of greatest extension, the ice sheet's peripheries could have been thermo-physically polar and sub-polar, as on the margins of today's Greenland ice sheet. But in their most regressive phases, the lower latitude margins were more than likely temperate, with only high interior sectors remaining "cold". Such combined conditions characterize a fifth thermo-physical category, which in the geophysical sense may be termed *polythermal*. To some extent all glaciers are polythermal, except in the final wasting temperate phase when they are fully isothermal.

To elucidate the characteristics of each of these five categories and to identify prototypes with suggested thermal parameters, selected field studies on existing glaciers are discussed and thermal measurements and characteristics illustrated. From the sampled data, arbitrary englacial temperature limits are suggested: for the main body of *polar glaciers* (-10 to $-70°C$); for *sub-polar glaciers* (-2 to $-10°C$); for *sub-temperate glaciers* (-0.1 to $-2°C$); for *temperate glaciers* (in summer, $0°C$ throughout); and for *polythermal glaciers* (a range across at least two of the foregoing temperature zones). The significance of thermal anomalies, temperature sandwich structures, diagenetic ice zones, and measured shifts in thermodynamic characteristics over a number of years are considered as they aid in the interpretation of ice morphology, glacier regimes, and climatic change.

Type thermo-physical examples are briefly compared from the following areas: the Antarctic and Greenland ice sheets (polar and polythermal), the Nepal Himalaya, Svalbard (polar to sub-polar). Lapland (sub-polar), sub-Arctic Norway (sub-temperate), the Juneau Icefield, Alaska (sub-temperate to temperate), the Alaskan-British Columbian coast (temperate), glacier systems on Mount Rainier, Washington State (polythermal), and icefields in the St Elias Mountains, Yukon Territory (temperate to polythermal).

The relationship of thermal anomalies is clarified and illustrated within the defined framework of each category. It is noted how these are manifest by deformation irregularities, differing salinities, and varying heat capacities within the ice. Also discussed is the relationship of changes in thermo-physical characteristics to the sensitivity of ice flow, revealed by changes in entropy and negentropy of glacier systems and by observable shifts from *parabolic to rectilinear* to *surging flow*. Finally considered is the long-term implication of secular changes in climate and their influences on englacial thermal regimes which affect the hydrological capacity and fluvial discharge of glaciers as well as their terminal fluctuations. The strong interdependence of all these factors and the total systems analysis which they represent underscore the mandate for a rational thermo-physical classification of glaciers.

Discussion

J. W. GLEN: I recognize that there are great complications in special cases; however, there are situations which are different from each other and for which it is worth finding a terminology to express the difference, as is the case for polar, sub-polar and temperate glaciers. This is surely helpful (e.g. for school textbooks). Just because there are blurred boundaries we do not cease to use the concepts of solid, liquid, and gas (for example, because such things as bouncing putty exist)!

For our purposes, however, it seems undesirable to try to categorize a large glacier which has various zones. Is it not better to follow Benson and discuss *facies* so that one glacier has various facies at various levels — and may have relics of other facies deeper down?

M. M. MILLER: Thank you for your comment that blurred boundaries need not preclude generalization of categories. As for the *polythermal* category, it is suggested only for general reference, and specifically in cases where insufficient information is in hand to delineate facies. Certainly the *polythermal* term must connote the existence of thermal or even water-content facies, and in the definition this should be well explained.

If we back up for a moment and look at this in a broader context, we can be reminded that the facies concept has been widely applied in geology, especially stratigraphy, for the handling of lateral, and to some extent vertical, changes in the lithologic character of sandstones, shales, limestones, etc. Such facies changes have considerable environmental significance with respect to provenance of the clastics involved. So, traditionally, I have had little difficulty in applying the environmental rationale to the thermal and physical "stratigraphy" of glaciers. Therefore, as in geology where the recognition and classification of rock facies do not vitiate reference to the main lithologic unit, why not in glaciology use a term which is applicable to the whole glacier unit, especially if one of our other suggested categories does not readily apply? In other words, if there is not a *dominantly polar* or *dominantly temperate* situation, call it *polythermal*, with all of the environmental, geophysical and orographical connotations. Such an application would simply recognize that indeed the unit comprises a *whole system of facies*, which actually is quite complex. (The separate identification of facies would then be left as a study in itself.) Perhaps one refinement could be to apply the *polythermal* term only to those cases which bridge the full range from polar to temperate, and not use it where the thermal range is less.

Again the aim has been to suggest a relatively simple classification, one which tries to remain consistent with previous terms yet which hopefully succeeds in identifying the dominant thermal character of the glacier system *as a whole*. If complications and uncertainties do not warrant this, then of course the segmental or facies concept could be more rigorously applied. And so the plea is not to overcomplicate the situation but, instead, through a rationally induced classification, to improve communication between scientists on these seemingly simple but at heart rather complex matters.

L. LLIBOUTRY: We need different classifications according to the goal in view. (For instance for case histories, an alphabetical classification would be the best one.) Thus I favour two distinct classifications: one, for studies of mass balance, relations with meteorology, etc., according to the thermal conditions in the firn (as developed by Shumskiy, F. Müller and others, etc.); and another, for glacier dynamics, where the bulk of the glacier (not the firn or a superficial thin layer getting cold in winter) is considered; namely, a temperate glacier with liquid water in it, and cold glaciers with a cold glacier – bedrock interface (no sliding), with a glacier – bedrock interface at the melting point, and with a temperate layer at the bottom. (I doubt whether this last case is Lagally's transitional glacier.)

MILLER: There certainly may be merit in some kinds of climatologically related studies to consider the firn pack as a separate entity from the main underlying mass of glacial ice, but I have endeavoured to avoid invoking unusual complications in the terminology. Instead, I have followed the idea of a classification which can cannote *mutually affected* characteristics of both the firn pack and its underlying ice as a stress-influenced *total system*.

(The stress here could be climatological or kinetic, or both.) As for strict considerations in glacier dynamics the main interest would be in deformation and mass transfer of the deep ice. I believe that the suggested classification does indeed lend itself to this, with any pertinent subsidiary characteristics, say in the bottom zone, being best considered not by single terminology but by appropriate modifying comments to be appended to the framework categories of the suggested classification.

G.K.C. CLARKE: I would like to speak on behalf of preserving a certain vagueness in terminology. It seems to me that the use of highly specific terms to describe the thermal structure of a glacier can be abused to imply that you have more information than your measurements support.

MILLER: I agree, to the extent that the classification which I have discussed does retain a certain desired looseness. As for implying more information than one has, this danger is implicit in the use of any descriptive phraseology. There will always be a need for scientific integrity in any reporting endeavour. But I am not too concerned about the danger of muddying the scientific waters too much here because after all the presentation of facts is what is judged. Perhaps if we are not sure at all of what the thermal character of a glacier system is we could indeed call it "crypto-thermal"!

Reprinted from
Journal of Glaciology 16:74, 297-300 (1976)
Vol. 16, No. 74, 1976
pp. 297-300

The outline might appear as follows:

THERMO-PHYSICAL CHARACTERISTICS OF GLACIERS
A. Main Argument
    1. Glaciers had been divided on thermo-physical characteristics.
        a. Polar or "cold" which is primarily subfreezing.
        b. Temperate or "warm" which is consistently at a pressure melting point below a winter chill layer.

2. Problems with this simple division.
   a. These types can occur in various locations (high or low altitude, arctic or subarctic latitude) and are based on characteristics, not location
   b. Earlier scholars recognized need for intermediate classes, first subpolar and now subtemperate or transitional related to the point of deglaciation or reglaciation of the ice sheet. The need is also evident for studies of the variation in large ice sheets.
3. The classification proposed,
   a. Polar glaciers ($-10°$ to $-70°$ C) — Antarctic, Greenland.
   b. Subpolar glaciers ($-2°$ to $-10°$ C) — Lapland.
   c. Subtemperate glaciers ($-0.1°$ to $-2°$ C — Norway.
   d. Temperate glaciers (in summer, $0°$ throughout) — Alps.
   e. Polythermal glaciers (a range across two of the preceding temperature zones) — Mt. Rainier.
4. Most glaciers are polythermal except when finally melting. Also there are many irregularities and changes, but the classification helps order them.

B. Discussion
1. These categories can be applied to various *facies* of a glacier, not to whole glaciers.
   a. But there may still be a dominant classification of a glacier as a whole. This classification helps a general definition.
2. Other classifications are advanced, such as those for historical purposes or for dealing with mass balance or glacier dynamics.
   a. But this classification seeks to avoid complication. It has a useful vagueness because many measures are imprecise.

The outline shows the two-part structure of the article and the fact that the second part is a response to criticism of the first. A summary might be as simple as:

A useful general classification of glacier is on thermo-physical characteristics: polar ($-10°$ to $-70°$ C), sub-polar ($-2°$ to $-10°$ C), subtemperate ($-0.1°$ to $-2°$ C), temperate (in summer, $0°$ C throughout), and poly-thermal (ranging across two of the preceding). These terms may apply to glaciers as a whole or to layers within a glacier.

The outline captures the form of the article and the fact that the classification is courting objection. Outlines tend to show the structure of a text and the relationships among ideas as well as its substance. You will often find that writing down the structure will help you remember. Doing so gives you both a content clue and a structural clue for your meaning. Some summaries do show the structure, but they need not, and in many of your studies the structure is as important as the content. Although they differ in what they record, outline and summary will both be useful to you when you write down information for yourself. They are not interchangeable, and when you decide which to use, you should base your decision on what you think you will need to remember.

HOW TO ORGANIZE INFORMATION IN WRITING REPORTS

4

In many courses you will receive information in lectures or from reading books or articles, going on field trips, or performing laboratory experiments; then you will have to prepare a written report on the work you have done. The requirements for the report will demand that you do more than simply repeat the information that you have gathered; you will have to organize the material in order to present it to your reader.

In this chapter, we will explain the structures of three major ways to organize information: Narrative or time-based organization which deals with events or actions; descriptive or space-based organization which deals with physical entities or relationships; and explanatory or logic-based organization which deals with ideas and concepts. In each of these you are asked to impose order on your material. The finished report presents both the material and your organization to your reader who will evaluate you not only on what you include or exclude, but on how you have organized it. Remember that you will be most successful if you clearly show both the material and the way you have organized it. The latter shows how clearly you can think.

Narrative and Process Orders

Chapter Two presents a chart of typical organizations; three of them are organizations based on a sense of time: narrative, process, and cause-effect. We will take up the first two in this chapter and the third in Chapter 5. Our reason for dividing them this way is that narrative and process organizations are relatively straightforward, but cause-effect requires more interpretation of the information on your part and is more complex.

Although we often think of narratives as stories or fiction, most narratives are nonfictional. You will write narratives or process papers on many occasions, such as when you have to give an account of an experiment, describe the events leading up to an historical turning point, discuss a person's life, prepare a case study, present the changes in thinking about some concept, or prepare a review of the research on a topic you are studying. All of these require narratives of one sort or another. The difference between a narrative paper and a paper describing a process is that narrative deals with particular events (one person's life). Process is usually more general (a report of an experiment) and is often presented as a set of steps to the reader so that the reader can do the same thing the writer did. An important criterion for judging your narrative or process paper is whether the reader can replicate either actually or mentally what you set forth. These examples show the difference:

Narrative

One event
singled out

The election of 1860, judged by its conse-quences, was *the most momentous* in Ameri-can History.

One group of
people

As *the Democrats* gathered in convention in Charleston, South Carolina, in April, most of the Southern delegates came with the deter-mination to adopt a platform providing for federal protection of slavery in the territories: that is an official endorsement of the principles

Definite articles

of the Dred Scott decision. *The* Western Dem-ocrats, arriving with bitter recollections of how Southern influence had blocked their legisla-tive demands in the recent Congress, were angered at the rule-or-ruin attitude of the Southerners. *The* Westerners hoped, however, to negotiate a face-saving statement on slavery so as to hold the party together. They vaguely endorsed popular sovereignty and proposed that all questions involving slavery in the ter-ritories be left up to the Supreme Court. When *the* convention adopted *the* Western platform, the delegations from eight lower South states withdrew from the hall. The remaining dele-gates then proceeded to the selection of a candidate. Stephen A. Douglas led on every ballot, but he could not muster the two-third majority (of the original number of delegates) required by the party rules. Finally the manag-ers adjourned the convention to meet again in Baltimore in June. At the Baltimore session, most of the Southerners reappeared, only to walk out again. The rest of the Southerners had assembled at Richmond. The rump convention at Baltimore nominated Douglas. The South-ern bolters at Baltimore and the men in Richmond nominated John C. Breckinridge of Kentucky.

A specific result

Sectionalism had at least divided the historic Democratic party. *There were now* two Demo-cratic candidates in the field, and although Douglas had supporters in the South and

47

> Breckinridge in the North, one was the nominee of the Northern Democrats and the other of the Southern Democrats.

Current, Richard N., T. Harry Williams & Frank Freidel. Fifth Edition American History: A Survey, Volume I: To 1877, *Alfred A. Knopf, New York, 1979, pp. 370–371.* (Italics added)

Process

THE STEPS OF PROGRAM DEVELOPMENT

Announcing the process

Computer programming is the task of developing a program. This task is not difficult, but it must be done carefully. It involves much more than just writing instructions. To use the computer effectively as a problem-solving tool, several program-development steps must be carried out. These steps are:

Listing of five steps

Defining the problem — describing the problem, the input data associated with the problem, and the desired results in everyday English as clearly and completely as possible.

Planning a solution algorithm — deciding how to proceed in solving the problem; breaking the task into specific operations that the computer can perform.

Coding the solution — writing a program to direct the computer in performing the operations identified in the solution algorithm.

Checking out the program — debugging and testing the solution algorithm, and its computer-program form of representation, to insure that the desired results are provided as output.

Completing the documentation — gathering and verifying all documents associated with the program and assembling them in a *run manual* that can be referred to by anyone needing to know about the program.

Indicating sequence

The first four of these steps are generally performed in sequence: definition is basic to planning a solution algorithm, which must occur before programming, which must be followed by debugging and testing. Developing a successful program may involve some backtracking to rethink and rework earlier steps; for example, during the coding phase, the professionals are emphasizing that program checkout should begin early in program development; it is both possible and desirable to detect and remove certain types of errors at the time of problem definition. Still others can be detected when formulating the solution algorithm. Documentation is a vital task, and it must be a continuing one. Concise, accurate documentation is required at each step in the program-development cycle.

Marilyn Bohl. A Guide for Programmers, *Prentice Hall, 1978, pp. 27–28.*

Beginning and Ending

The structure of narrative or process papers most often follows a sequence from beginning to end, earlier to later, or past to present. You generally follow a natural order in telling a joke or giving an accident report. Imagine trying to make sense of the frames in a daily comic strip if the paper printed them out of order, and you will see how vital correct sequence can be. One problem you face, however, is to decide what the beginning and ending point should be. Let us suppose you have been given the assignment to describe the sequence of events leading up to the Civil War. If you think about it, you could begin with the election of Abraham Lincoln, but there are other events before that: the campaign of 1860, the Missouri Compromise, the Abolitionist movement, the invention of the cotton gin, the failure to address the issue of slavery in the Constitution, the slave trade, the patterns of settlement in America, and the Reformation. Which should you choose? One answer might be given in the assignment, but oftentimes the decision is yours. Two rules are clear: Start with the first event that you think is important and make clear why this is a good starting point.

The first rule should be followed quite rigidly. If you don't, you will irritate the reader by interrupting the flow of information with a phrase like "But earlier you must remember that. . . ." At times, of course, you may need to refer to earlier trends, but generally such a phrase gives the reader the impression that you forgot something and makes you look poorly organized.

The second rule has a bit more latitude than the first. You may simply have to state that you picked this point of history because you are dealing with events and not psychological or political reasons (these are more a matter of interpretation and are therefore debatable). Or you may want to say a bit more about why you are not going back further. Being as arbitrary as you want is all right; often common sense can help you. If you have the task of describing an experiment, you don't need to tell about climbing the stairs to the laboratory, but convention usually dictates that you start with the equipment, apparatus, subjects, or problems. This convention asserts what is relevant about experiments to readers.

Common sense and convention can tell you when to stop as well. You should stop either at the point assigned, such as the outbreak of hostilities in the Civil War, or when you have completed the report on the results of your experiment. Remember that you are more or less telling a story, and a good story has a climax and a terminal point. Of course, events do not stop at the climax. If you have performed a psychological experiment with some other students, they might go off afterward and think about it, but for you and your reader the experiment is over.

One example of a conventional process series is a recipe. The recipe begins with the ingredients, and ends when the dish is ready to eat. Although the recipe might include serving hints, how people ate it and whether or not they got indigestion are not relevant to the recipe.

Other conventional process papers include:

The psychological experiment:

> Statement of problem
> Subjects
> Treatment
> Results
> Interpretation

The biographical essay:

> Parents
> Birth and childhood
> Education
> Early career
> Triumph or defeat
> Aftermath and death
> Judgement by others

The review of research:

> Earliest conception of problem
> Changes in that conception
> Current conception

Making the Process Clear to the Reader

One of the most important things to remember in writing narrative or process papers, as in writing any composition, is that you must make clear to your reader the organization and relationships of the ideas or events as well as the nature of the ideas or events themselves. You need to signal the structure of your composition. Such signaling is the key to successful writing. In Chapter 2, we indicated certain words, phrases, or graphics that signal a narrative or process composition. The following chart elaborates these signals and divides them into four groups: those which indicate the *beginning*, those which show *continuity* of events, those

Table 4-1

WORDS		PHRASES	GRAPHICS
Beginning Signals			
first		as a start	A
before		the first step	I
beginning		at the first	I
starting		in the past	*Background*
		the purpose of	
		to begin with	
Continuing Signals			
next	after	in addition	*B, C, D*
then	later	a short time later	*II, III, IV*
following	again	long after	*2, 3, 4*
moreover	thence	in the next (seconds)	
afterwards	during		
ensuing	intervening		
Parallel Signals			
meanwhile		at the same time	[double columns]
while		parallel to	
as			
when			
Ending Signals			
finally		at the end	*Results*
thus		at the conclusion	*Discussion*
thence		at last	
now		to conclude	
today		to finish	
		to end	
		the final	
		lead to	
		result in	

which tell readers you are giving at least *one parallel set of events* (events happening at the same time), and those which indicate you are near *the end*. In some cases, these are synonymous words or phrases, but some are more formal than others. We will discuss the choices between more and less formal expressions in Chapter 6.

Descriptive Orders

Certain kinds of material that you may have to organize or reorganize do not change over time very much, but people think of how they are arranged in space. People use maps, charts, flow charts, diagrams, and symbols of various sorts in order to show relationships of tangible or physical objects such as cities or buildings or people's bodies. Sometimes, however, spatial organization may be less easy to see. You can create a "conceptual map" to describe the relationship of ideas, or states, or social organization. A chart showing the organization of government will put the President in the top box, the cabinet in boxes under the President, and on down to smaller and smaller boxes. This chart does not mean that the President is literally on the top floor of a building and the various subordinates on the floors below in descending order. The physical or spatial description is an analogy to a relationship of command or delegation of responsibility — of who reports to whom.

Whether physical or conceptual, a fair amount of academic writing describes relationships in spatial terms, as the following examples show.

Physical Relationships

Many of the body's reactions that result from activity of the autonomic nervous system are produced by the action of that system on the endocrine glands [see Figure 4-1]. The endocrine glands secrete *hormones* that are carried throughout the body by the bloodstream. These chemicals are as essential as the nervous system to the integration of the organism's activities and to the

Chapter 4

Figure 4-1   Some of the Endocrine Glands

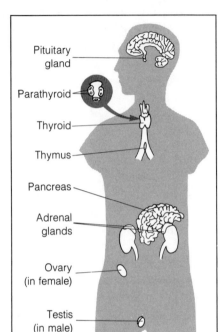

Pituitary gland

Parathyroid

Thyroid

Thymus

Pancreas

Adrenal glands

Ovary (in female)

Testis (in male)

From *Introduction to Psychology*, Eighth Edition by Rita L. Atkinson, Richard C. Atkinson and Ernest R. Hilgard, copyright © 1983 by Harcourt Brace Jovanovich, Inc. Reprinted and reproduced by permission of the publisher.

maintenance of *homeostasis*. Some endocrine glands are controlled by the nervous system, whereas others respond to the internal state of the body.

One of the major endocrine glands, the *pituitary*, is partly an outgrowth of the brain and is joined to it just below the hypothalamus and thereby under the control of other brain centers via the hypothalamus. The pituitary gland has been called the "master gland" because it produces the largest number of different hormones and controls the secretion of several other endocrine glands. One of the pituitary hormones has the crucial job of controlling body growth. Too little of this hormone can create a dwarf, while oversecretion can produce a giant. A number of other hormones released by the pituitary trigger the action of other endocrine glands such as the thyroid, the sex glands, and the outer layer of the adrenal gland. Courtship, mating, and reproductive behavior in many animals is based on a complex interaction between the activity of the nervous system and the influence of the pituitary on the sex glands.

The *adrenal glands* play an important role in determining an individual's mood, level of energy, and ability to cope with stress. Each adrenal gland has two parts, an inner core and an outer layer. The inner core secretes *epinephrine* (also known as *adrenalin*) and *norepinephrine* (*noradrenalin*). Epinephrine acts in a number of ways to prepare the organism for an emergency; it often works in conjunction with the sympathetic division of the autonomic nervous system.

Atkinson, Atkinson, Hilgard. Introduction to Psychology *8th Ed. San Diego, Harcourt Brace Jovanovich 1983, p. 53.*

Conceptual Relationships

A simple system flowchart is shown in Figure 4-2. The *process symbol* (□) tells us that a monthly billing program is to be written and executed; the *punched-card symbol* (▱) indicates that input (quantity and unit price) is to be entered on punched cards; and the *document symbol* (▱) indicates that output (amount due) is to be printed on a paper document. The direction of data flow is shown by *flowlines*. We cannot tell by looking at Figure 4-2 whether multiplication, addition, subtraction, or a combination of these operations is needed to compute monthly bills. We cannot tell the order in which required operations must be performed. To provide this detailed information, the programmer constructs a program flowchart.

In contrast to a system flowchart, a program flowchart (also called a *block diagram or logic diagram*) shows the detailed

Figure 4-2   **System Flowchart for Monthly Billing**

processing steps within one computer program and the sequence in which those steps must be executed. (A system flowchart may show the flow of data through several programs, but each process symbol on a system flowchart represents one program.) To emphasize this distinction, a program flowchart showing the detailed processing steps in the monthly billing program and the system flowchart for the program are shown in Figure 4-3.

The program shown in Figure 4-3 controls the sequence of operations required to prepare a monthly statement for one customer. *Terminal symbols* (⊂⊃) show clearly the beginning and ending of the program. The computer performs reading and writing as well as calculations. Note that the process and flowline symbols are used on both system and program flowcharts. Specialized input/output symbols appear on the system flowchart, but the *generalized input/output symbol* (▱) is used on the program flowchart. As mentioned above, the major emphasis of a program flowchart is on the detailed operations performed on data, not on the media or devices used. Use of the specialized input/output symbols would tend to distract readers from its main purpose. Furthermore, modern EDP systems often permit devices to be assigned at program execution time, taking into account the devices available at that time. For these reasons, use of specialized input/output symbols on program flowcharts is not recommended. Either generalized or specialized input/output symbols may appear on system flowcharts. Because the system flowchart is intended to show the forms of input and output, use of specialized input/output symbols is usually preferred.

Marilyn Bohl, A Guide for Programmers, *Prentice Hall, 1978, p. 66.*

The structure of descriptive writing follows a set of conventions adapted from our common sense about space. You probably describe objects located in space using one or more of these adjectives:

> horizontal — from left to right or right to left (side to side)
> vertical — from top to bottom or bottom to top (up and down)

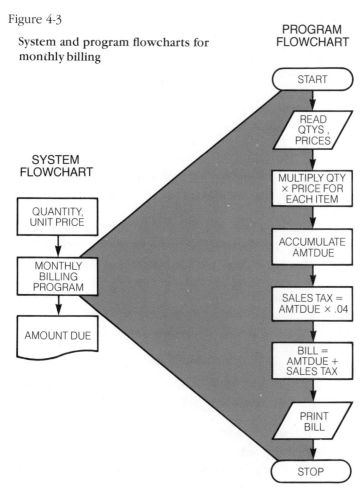

Conceptual Relationships

Figure 4-3

System and program flowcharts for monthly billing

PROGRAM FLOWCHART

START

READ QTYS, PRICES

SYSTEM FLOWCHART

QUANTITY, UNIT PRICE

MULTIPLY QTY × PRICE FOR EACH ITEM

MONTHLY BILLING PROGRAM

ACCUMULATE AMTDUE

AMOUNT DUE

SALES TAX = AMTDUE × .04

BILL = AMTDUE + SALES TAX

PRINT BILL

STOP

Marilyn Bohl, *A Guide For Programmers*, © 1978, pp. 27–28, 66, 67. Reprinted by permission of Prentice-Hall, Inc., Englewood Cliffs, New Jersey.

penetrating—from inside to outside or outside to inside (through)

circular—from one point on a circumference to another (around) perspective—from front to back or back to front (towards or away)

traveling—following the writer's path as the writer moves from place to place (moving)

As you write a description, you should first indicate to your reader which structure or descriptive order you are going to use. This will help the reader see things as you do.

Next you should use words that clearly indicate the physical relationship among the objects or concepts that you are describing as in Table 4-2. You can see that some of the words used to indicate spatial relationships are derived from narratives ("starting," "ending," "next"). The reason for this seeming confusion is that writers are leading readers through visual space but doing so in a time sequence. They want readers to begin somewhere and end somewhere. You can also see that some of the terms, like *next* or *above* are used in several orderings. It is for that reason among others that you, the writer, could clearly show the reader the direction you want to have followed. A sentence like "The building is near the park" does not give any clue as to the direction, only as to the relative distance. "The building is to the left of the park as you face the West entrance" gives the clues.

In many descriptions, a writer will use more than one orientation. The reason for this combining is that we live in a world of three dimensions and a description is frequently of either a two-dimensional or a three-dimensional object, as in the following example:

> He was called Jacopo Robusti, nicknamed Tintoretto (1518-94). He too had tired of the simple beauty of forms and colours which Titian had shown to the Venetians—but his discontent must have been more than a mere desire to accomplish the unusual. He seems to have felt that, however incomparable Titian was as

Table 4-2 STRUCTURAL SIGNALS
FOR DESCRIPTIVE COMPOSITION

General terms to begin and end

starting	ending
beginning	terminating

Horizontal

from the	moving to the (right, left)
next to	on the (right, left)
beside	on the (right, left) side of
	to the

Vertical

from	to	downward
above	below	upper
underneath	next (above, below)	lower
going (up/down)	upward	

Penetrating

on the inside	on the surface
at the center	on the edge
at the middle	outer
at the core	deeper
inner	below
next	above
outward	radially across the radius, diameter
inward	at a point on the radius, diameter
on the outside	

Circular

clockwise	north
counterclockwise	south
east	west
next to the	on the perimeter

Perspective

behind	middle	far
in back of	in front of	toward
in the background	in the foreground	away from
near		

Traveling

go	look	follow
walk	notice	trace
turn	stop	continue

a painter of beauty, his pictures tended to be more pleasing than moving: that they were not sufficiently exciting to make the great stories of the Bible and the sacred legends live for us. Whether he was right in this or not, he must, at any rate, have been resolved to tell these stories in a different way, to make the spectator feel the thrill and tense drama of the events he painted. ["The Finding of Saint Mark's Remains"] shows that he did indeed succeed in making his pictures unusual and captivating. At first glance this painting looks confused and confusing. Instead of a clear arrangement of the main figures *in the plane* of the picture, such as Raphael had achieved, we look *into the depths* of a strange vault. There is a tall man with a halo at the *left corner*, raising his arm as if to stop something that is happening — and if we follow his gesture we can see that he is concerned with what is going on *high up under* the roof of the vault on the *other side* of the picture. There are two men about to lower a dead body from a tomb — they have lifted its lid — and a third man in a turban is helping them, while a nobleman *in the background* with a torch is trying to read the inscription on another tomb. These men are evidently plundering a catacomb. One of the bodies is stretched out on a carpet in strange foreshortening, while a dignified old man in a gorgeous costume kneels *beside* it and looks at it. *In the right corner* there is a group of men and women, apparently frightened and looking with astonishment at the saint — for a saint the figure with the halo must be. If we look more closely we see that he carries a book — he is St. Mark the Evangelist, the patron saint of Venice — which reminds us that the dignified old man wears the robe of a Venetian Doge.

Establishes three-dimensions

Left indicates horizontal

Vertical
Horizontal

Gombrich, E. H. The Story of Art, *Phaidon Publishers, Inc., Garden City Books, New York, MCMLII, pp. 270–271.* (Italics added)

Logic-based Organizations

In addition to arranging material you write about in narrative and descriptive orders, frequently you will be asked to analyze this material. Usually what is meant by this assignment is that you should "take apart" the material, show what it is or what it is made up of. In the first instance you are defining the material — separating it from other similar objects or ideas. In the second instance you are classifying the material — arranging its parts into some sort of logical set of divisions.

Definition by example

The world is full of so many different objects that if we treated each one as distinct, we would soon be overwhelmed. For example, if we had to refer to every different object we encountered by a different name our vocabulary would have to be gigantic — so gigantic that communication would be impossible (we probably would not remember most of the words). Fortunately, we do not teach each object as unique but as an instance of a class or concept. Thus, many different objects are seen as instances of the concept *apple*, many others as instances of the concept *chair*, and so on. By treating many different objects as if they were roughly the same or the same with respect to certain properties, we reduce the complexity of the world to manageable proportions.

Definition

To have a concept is to know the properties common to all or most instances of the concept. Thus, our concept of *apple* consists of properties shared by most apples — that they are edible, have seeds, grow on trees, are round, have distinctive colors, and so on. Knowledge of these common properties has an enormous impact on how we deal with the objects around us. Having perceived some visible properties of an object — something round and red on a tree — we assign it to the concept of *apple*. This allows us to infer properties that are not visible — for instance, that it has seeds and is edible. Concepts, then, enable us to go beyond the information we perceive. This ability is fundamental to thought.

Definition by function

Often we do not have to perceive the properties of an object or a person to know much about it. If you are introduced to a doctor you immediately know he or she has a medical degree, extensive knowledge about disease, and experience with patients. You do not have to see any of these properties directly; you can infer them indirectly from the concept of *doctor*. Concepts, then, allow us to apply what we already know — the common properties of a doctor or an apple — to people and objects we encounter for the first time.

We also have concepts of activities, such as *eating*; of states, such as *being old*; and of abstract things, such as *truth, justice,* or even the number *two*. In each case, we know something about the properties common to members of the concept. Widely used concepts like these generally are associated with a one-word name: "apple," "doctor," "eating," "old," "truth," and so forth. This allows us to communicate quickly about things that occur frequently. Such concepts are the major concern of this section.

Classical and probabilistic concepts

Classification

Distinction

Class 1

We have talked about the common properties of a concept as if every property in a concept were true of every possible instance. Although some concepts, called *classical*, are like this, other concepts, called *probabilistic*, are not. An example of a classical concept is a *bachelor*; every instance of this concept must have the properties of being adult, male, and unmarried. If someone described an adult as a *married bachelor*, you would probably

Class 2

think that person did not really understand the concept of bachelor. An example of a probabilistic concept is *bird*. Even though most people's concept of bird includes the properties of flying and chirping, not all birds fly (ostriches and penguins do not) and not all birds chirp (ducks, crows, and chickens do not). So, if someone talked about a *nonflying bird,* you would find it perfectly acceptable. Most of our everyday concepts seem to be probabalistic (Smith and Medin, 1981).

For probabilistic concepts, some instances will have more of the concept's properties than other instances. Among birds, for example, a robin will have the property of flying, whereas an ostrich will not. And the more properties of a concept that an instance has, the more typical people consider that instance to be of the concept. Thus, people rate a robin as more typical of *bird* than an ostrich, they rate red apples as more typical than green ones of *apple* (since red seems to be a property of the concept *apple*), and so on. Not only do people judge one instance of a concept to be more typical than the other, they also classify the more typical one faster. The question "Is a robin a bird?" produces an immediate "yes"; "Is a chicken a bird?" takes longer. In addition to being classified faster, typical instances are more accessible in memory than less typical ones; when asked to list all the birds they can think of, people produce robin before ostrich (Rosch, 1978).

Subclass of 2

Concepts about people are usually probabilistic and may contain numerous properties that are not true of all instances. Consider the concept *computer scientist*. Some properties — such as *knows how to program a computer* — are usually true of all members of the concept; others — such as *has a need for order and clarity* — are at best only characteristic of some members. Yet, if you were given a brief description of a person and told only that he or she had a need for order, you would be far more likely to think that the person was in computer science than, say, in education or social work. When we make such decisions, we are essentially dealing in stereotypes (Kahneman, Slovic, and Tversky, 1982).

Typicality has important implications for mental life. When we think of a concept, we are likely to think of a typical instance of it. Consider an example. Away from home, you feel ill and think about seeing a doctor. You cannot be thinking of a specific doctor (you do not know one there) but rather must be dealing with the concept *doctor*. Your concept fits some doctors (probably those who are middle-aged and male) better than others. Why? Because most doctors you have seen, either directly or through the media, have been middle-aged males. These properties have become part of your concept. If Doctor Jones turns out to be young and female, you will be surprised. Our thoughts and expectations, then, are biased in important ways. Since they are based on experience, however, presumably they can be changed by experience. As more and more women become doctors, our concepts of doctors should change.

Atkinson, Atkinson & Hilgard, Introduction to Psychology, *pp. 254–255.*

The Structures of Definition and Classification

What your reader sees when you define or classify does not usually represent the procedure you followed to arrive at your definition or classification. A definition often begins with an opening like "Thermodynamics may be defined as ..." and a classification with one like "Social behavior may be divided into three basic types ..." Both formats start with a general statement and move through an orderly series of progressively specific material. The structure is like that of the parlor game "Twenty Questions" where the players begin with "animal, vegetable, or mineral" and divide the broad category further with each succeeding question. To play the game successfully, if the object is animal, you should ask each question so that it divides the universe in half. "Is it a real animal?" "Yes." "Is it a living animal?" Each successive division narrows the universe.

But when people *begin* to classify material — objects, events, or ideas — they start the other way, with a large number of specifics that they have to put into some order. Successful writers start making lists and determining what items belong together in groups. The number of groups may vary, but the groupings are usually such that a particular item can go into only one group, and there is only a very small miscellaneous category, if any. These groups of fairly specific items are then grouped into larger groups, and the larger ones into larger ones until, if you are thinking about "Twenty Questions," you would end up with *animal*. We have found, by the way, that making lists is one of the best ways to prepare for most academic compositions — not just classifications. If the assignment is to define a concept like "social system," a good starting point is to make a list of aspects of a social system or a list of other people's definitions to help order your own thoughts.

Of course, the list is not what you hand in; the composition should be almost the reverse of the process you have gone through in getting ready to write. In both a definition and a classification, you start with the broadest category or the broadest definition and successively narrow things down.

Structure of Classification

The structure of a classification is relatively straightforward. After indicating what you are going to classify, you indicate the basis of the classes, list each class, and conclude with a sentence or two about any items that do not fit the classification. That was the structure of the paper on glaciers in Chapter 3 (p. 37 – 42). It is the structure of the following classification of love.

Introduces classification *First subset*	At this point I wish to teach you about the *three* stages of love: nascent, declared and consummated. *Nascent love* is that tenderness first conceived in the hearts of man or woman, the beginning of a mutual sympathy and desire. *Declared love* is affection openly offered and accepted by both — that singleness of will that one feels when the man becomes the lady's special friend, and she his.
Second subset	
Third subset	*Consummated love* is reached when the desires of both achieve complete fulfillment in kiss and embrace. There are those, too, who would say that there exists a *fourth stage* of love, namely *permanent love*, which leads to a marriage sanctified by the sacraments of the holy church. But whatever they say, I insist that such is not properly a stage of the love here under discussion. For married love is like a debt which one must pay, while the love of which I speak is a kind of grace freely bestowed. Although it is a mark of good manners to pay what one owes, still, there is no more delightful love than that born of the gratuitous favor of an artless, ingenuous heart.
Fourth subset rejected	
Second classification and summary of classes	Since you now know the three stages of love, you must learn also that in love there are *three kinds* of sickness. The first is known as the "lovesick fever." The second is the "restless affliction"; and the third, the "transform-

First subset   ing disease." "*Lovesick fever*" is an illness that befalls those newly afflicted with a yearning heart. That is, when one takes it into his mind to love, and must debate with himself whether he shall do so or not; and if so, how he shall go about it. Such reflections chase all other thoughts and desires from his mind. They rob him of all appetite, sleep and repose, until, at length, he begins to grow pale, just as if he were suffering from a veritable

Second subset   fever. The "*restless affliction*" is a sickness that lovers must endure when they cannot long remain in one place, but wish, rather, to go again and again where their heart longs to be. And there are some who jokingly call this

Third subset   sickness "Saint James's disease." The "*transforming disease*" is the illness that lovers suffer when they seem to have lost their memory and mind; for they lose all sense of proper behavior and bearing, and shun the company of one and all, wishing no other solace than the thought of their love. These, then, are the three kinds of lovesickness. Perhaps some will ask, if love is as excellent a quality as I have stated, and the seat of so many noble virtues, how it can be that one finds within it such pain and heartache.

De Fournival, Richard. Advice on Love, *Chapter in* The Comedy of Eros Medieval French Guides to the Art of Love, *University of Illinois Press, Urbana, IL, 1971, pp. 112–114.* (Italics added)

Notice that the author uses a three-part classification in each paragraph. He announces what the classes are and then proceeds to expand each class. The signals he uses are quite obvious and follow the procedures in Table 4-3. In his first paragraph, De Fournival also shows why he excludes one class.

Table 4-3   STRUCTURAL SIGNALS
                   FOR CLASSIFICATION

Introductory

divided into   composed of
made up of   constituted of
consists of   : (colon)
comprises

Separators

first, second, third   subset
A, B, C   separate from
1, 2, 3   distinct from
sub-species   differs

Concluders

constitute
make up

Structure of Definition

The organization of your definition might follow one of the
structures listed in Table 4-4. In a paper which is primarily
devoted to definition, you might use more than one of the
systems of definition, and you probably should, but you
should try to keep each system distinct — one system to a
paragraph — and tell your reader how you are defining the
object, as the following ancient example demonstrates.

Origin   Adam gave their name to CAMELS (camelis)
                  with good reason, for when they are being
                  loaded up they kneel down and make them-
                  selves lower or humbler — and the Greek for
                  low or humble is *'cam'*. Or else it is because
                  the creature is humped on the back and the
                  word *'camur'* means 'curved' in Greek.

Location   Although other regions produce them, yet
                  Arabia does so most. The Bactrians breed the
                  strongest camels, but Arabia breeds the

Table 4-4   WORDS SIGNALING
                   A STRATEGY OF DEFINITION

DEFINITION BY:

Example

instance of	cite
example of	name
version of	case of
occurs when	the name for

Analogy

like	compared to
resembles	as

Separation, contrast, or elimination

is distinct from	unlike
differs from	not
is not like	

Location

occurs	in
seems	when
finds itself	

Amplification and repetition

called	denominated
referred to	labelled
named	is

Origin, cause, or effect

begins	results in
results from	derived from
the cause of	named by
caused by	

Amplifications

largest number. The two kinds differ in this, that the Arabians have humps on the back.

These Bactrians never wear away their hoofs. They have fleshy soles with certain concertina-like pads, and from these there is a cushioning counteraction for the walkers, with no hard impediment to putting down the foot.

They are kept for two purposes. Some are accommodated to carry a burden. Others are more speedy, but cannot be given loads beyond what is fitting, nor are the latter willing to do more than the accustomed distances.

When they come into season, they are so unbridled by the matter that they run mad for want of love.

They detest horses.

They are good at putting up with the weariness of thirst, and indeed, when the chance of drinking is given them, they fill up with enough both for the past want and for whatever lack may come in the future for a long time. They go for dirty waters and avoid clean ones. In fact, unless there should be fouler drink available, they themselves stir up the slime with busy trampling, in order that it should be muddied.

They live for a hundred years.

If they happen to be sold to a stranger they grow ill, disgusted at the price.

Females are provided in warfare, but it is so arranged that their desire for copulation is frustrated: for they are thought to do more valiantly if they are prevented from coition.

White, T. H. (Editor) The Bestiary: A Book of Beasts *being a translation from* A Latin Bestiary of the Twelfth Century. *Capricorn Books, G. P. Putman's Sons, New York, 1960, pp. 79–80.*

The advantage of several types of definition as opposed to one can be seen if one compares the definition of a camel with the following briefer definition of what we must suppose is a bison from the same volume.

An animal is born in Asia which they call a BONNACON, and he has a bullish head and from then on the rest of his body like a horse's mane. The horns are curled round upon themselves with such a multiple convolution that if anybody bumps against them he does not get hurt.

But however much his front end does not defend this monster, his belly end is amply sufficient. For when he turns to run away he emits a fart with the contents of his large intestine which covers three acres. And any tree that it reaches catches fire. Thus he drives away his pursuers with noxious excrement.

White, The Bestiary, *33.*

HOW TO ORGANIZE WHAT YOU THINK AND EXPRESS WHAT YOU MEAN: HOW TO CONVINCE YOUR READER (I.E., PROFESSOR) THAT WHAT YOU THINK AND EXPRESS IS VALID

5

Perhaps the most demanding and rewarding kind of writing you will be asked for will not require you simply to copy material or to *impose* an order on it (such as classify it). Instead you will have to *create* a *new* order for the material. You will have to interpret the material, think about it, and present it to the audience in a *form* that lets them see it as you do. A part of your task lies in your thinking; another part lies in presenting your thoughts so that you convince your audience of the validity of those thoughts. Some people refer to interpretive writing as argument—not in the sense of quarrelling—but in the sense of persuading readers to admit that yours is a reasonable interpretation. Generally readers will accept your thesis if you provide solid evidence and a sound structure. They will have a hard time saying, "Yes, but..." In this chapter we will discuss three general structures of interpretive writing: comparison and contrast, cause and effect, and thesis support. Preparing papers that have one or more of these three structures will be a part of many assignments in your courses.

Comparison-Contrast

Many academic assignments require that you look at two pieces of material and compare them. Many students misinterpret the assignment and assume that comparison means only similarities, but it also means differences. A comparison includes a contrast, and a contrast includes a comparison, as the following example by a British linguist shows.

Linguistics is descriptive, not prescriptive
The term *descriptive* is here being employed in a different sense from the sense in which it opposes either *general*, on the one hand, or *historical*, on the other. The *contrast that is relevant* here is the one that holds between **describing** how things are and **prescribing** how things ought to be. An alternative to 'prescriptive', in the sense in which it contrasts with 'descriptive', is 'normative'. To say that linguistics is a descriptive (i.e. non–normative) science is to say that the linguist *tries to discover and record* **the rules** to which the members of a language-community actually conform and *does not seek to impose* upon them **other (i.e. extraneous) rules, or norms**, of correctness.

The contrast established

The comparative point

Redefinition to establish contrast

It is perhaps confusing to use the term 'rule', as I have just done, in these two very different senses. Rightly or wrongly, linguists talk in these terms. It might be helpful, therefore, to illustrate the difference between the two kinds of rules — let us call them immanent and transcendent, respectively — from

The contrast

An analogy to establish the contrastive principle

something other than the use of language. Let us take sexual behaviour in a given society. If we adopt the purely descriptive (i.e. non-normative) point of view in the investigation of sexual behaviour, we will try to find out how people actually behave: whether they practice premarital sex, and, if so, of what kind and from what age; whether husbands and wives are equally faithful or unfaithful to their partners; and so on. In so far as the behaviour of particular groups within the community is governed, in practice, by determinable principles — whether the members of these groups profess, or are even aware of, these principles or not — we can say that their behaviour is rule-governed: the rules are **immanent** in their actual behaviour. But such rules (if they are rightly called rules) are very different, in status if not in content, from the rules of conduct that the law, the established religion or simply explicit conventional morality might prescribe. People may or may not conform, in practice, to what I am calling the **transcendent** (i.e. extraneous or nonimmanent) rules of sexual behaviour. Furthermore, there may be differences between how they behave and how they say, or even think, that they behave. All these differences have their correlates in respect of language-behaviour. The most important distinction, however, is the one that holds between transcendent (i.e. prescriptive) and immanent (i.e. descriptive) rules. Prescriptive *dos* and *don'ts* are commands (*Do/Don't say X!*); descriptive *dos* and *don'ts* are statements (*People do/don't say X*).

Back to linguists

The reason why present-day linguists are so insistent about the distinction between descriptive and prescriptive rules is simply that traditional grammar is very strongly normative in character. The grammarian saw it as his task to formulate the standards of correctness and to impose these, if necessary, upon the speakers of the language. Many of the normative precepts of traditional grammar will be familiar to the reader: "You should never use a double-negative" (*I didn't do nothing*); "Don't end a sentence with a preposition" (*That's the man I was speaking to*); "The verb 'to be' takes the same case after it as before" (so that, by the application of this rule, "*It's me* should be corrected to *It is I*); "*Ain't* is wrong": "You should not split the infinitive" (as in *I want you to clearly understand* where *clearly* is inserted between *to* and *understand*).

John Lyons. Language and Linguistics: An Introduction. *Cambridge, England, Cambridge University Press, 1981, pp. 47–49.* (Italics added)

The author first establishes a contrast between description and prescription and also immediately shows they have rules in common. Using the analogy of sexual behavior, he distinguishes the two meanings or uses of rules. To make the contrast, then, the writer has to establish some point of common ground, a reason for comparing and contrasting the ideas, events, or objects. Comparison-contrast is the interpretive side of classification; a classification paper puts ideas in groups. The author who writes the reasons for putting two items in the same group or different groups creates a comparison-contrast paper. Lyons had to justify why he divided rules into descriptive and prescriptive; and he did so by contrasting the two and comparing the contrast in linguistics to a contrast in social behavior. You might be asked to classify plants and divide them into trees and shrubs. Then you would need to show the differences and explain why neither are vines. The result would be a comparison-contrast because you had to interpret and not just organize the data.

A Procedure for Comparing and Contrasting

Let us suppose you received the assignment of comparing two short stories. The first step would be to make a double column list of similarities and differences. We can use a comparison of *Little Red Riding Hood* and *Cinderella* as an example.

	LITTLE RED RIDING HOOD	CINDERELLA
Similarities:		
	traditional	
	hero is female	
	ends happily	
	includes deception	
	includes recognition scene	

	LITTLE RED RIDING HOOD	CINDERELLA
Differences:	young girl	older
	parent alive	parent dead
	escapes danger	gets husband
	wolf is deceiver	Cinderella is deceiver
	setting rural	setting urban
	physical violence	psychological violence
	no magic	magic
	one event	three events

Note that some items are not on the list — such as the fact that both stories use words or that both have gone through many revisions or that both have been made into films. These points of similarity are normal and therefore not as important as the fact that one has more incidents than the other, a significant point of difference. You should exclude these or other similarities or differences for one of two reasons. First, any two things that are compared may have in common the characteristics that put them in a large class such as *story*. The large class provides the reason for even considering a comparison. The real question, however, is whether they belong in the same sub-class — you will have to justify the answer. The second reason is that common sense tells us that no two items are exactly alike and that some differences are appropriate on some occasions and not on others. A person might have high-heeled shoes and low-heeled shoes and might have brown shoes and black shoes. On one occasion the difference in heels might determine which will be worn; color will be immaterial; on another occasion color will be the important determinant; heel length will not matter.

In the case of the stories then, the fact that the tales are traditional and contain heroines establishes a reason for pairing them. But are they really in the same category or sub-class? In some respects they are: both have a deception and a recognition. But the deceptions are different — the girl is deceived in one and is the deceiver in the other. The recognitions are the climax of each story.

As you look at the differences, you will want to relate some differences to the apparent similarities. Both have female main characters, but are they the same? Both end happily, but is the result the same? And so on down the list.

Now the final part of the task is to decide whether the similarities outweigh the differences. Do the two stories belong in the same sub-class? Probably not. And the reasons would form the major argument of your paper.

The Structure of Comparison-Contrast

A comparison-contrast composition is marked by one of two structures: an all-about-A, all-about-B structure or a pendulum structure. In the first structure you list all the pertinent features of one and then all the features of the other in a parallel fashion. This structure is often used, but it usually places a greater burden on your reader who has to remember the features of one while you give the features of the second. It is best used when you have only a few features to discuss or if you are doing the comparison-contrast in a paragraph or two. In the pendulum structure you take one aspect of similarity and difference and describe how it applies to each of the two, then go to another aspect, and another until you are through. This structure signals clearly the point of similarity or difference and elaborates how the similarity or difference operates. The two examples that follow show the two structures.

SIMILARITY USING OBJECT-ONE/OBJECT-TWO

Object-one:
The boy's hooting

The first, preliminary sampling comes in Book V, in the passage on the boy of Winander, published separately in 1800 as "There Was a Boy." Wordsworth first wrote the lines as autobiography; then, changing them to the third person, he added sentimental lines on the boy's death and his own meditations beside the grave. The lines stand in the *Prelude* in this weakened form. But we are told in taut lines how the boy hooted in mimicry of owls and listened for their answering calls. In the unanswering silence that sometimes ensued, he felt suddenly deep within, the "solemn imagery" of the torrents, rocks, woods, and, in Wordsworth's magnificent metaphor for the reflection of drifting clouds, "that uncertain Heaven, receiv'd Into the bosom of the steady Lake." In this paradox of steady liquid made to appear unsteady by its acceptance of heaven, Wordsworth asserts yet once again the divine unity of sky and water, known and felt through the imagination. The boy deliberately exerted energy, waited tensely, began to relax, and felt suddenly the enduring power of Nature. Wordsworth described this sequence circumstantially in his Preface of 1815: "The Boy, there introduced, is listening, with something of a feverish and restless anxiety, for the recurrence of the riotous sounds which he had previously excited; and, at the moment when the intenseness of his mind is beginning to remit, he is surprized into a perception of the solemn and tranquillizing images which the Poem describes."

Object-two:
The man at the
road

De Quincey, in "Literary Reminiscences," informs us that Wordsworth traced a parallel sequence through an episode when he awaited important news. After long tension, with his ear to the road to catch the first sound of wheels, he abandoned hope, raised his head with relaxed senses, and perceived suddenly a bright star, which brought to him "a pathos and a sense of the Infinite." Make of this as little as you can; call it vertigo: The imprint of the experience on the moral being remains the same.

Carl Woodring. Wordsworth, Riverside Studies in Literature, *Gordon N. Ray (Ed.), Houghton Mifflin Company, Boston, 1965, pp. 110–111.*

Contrast Using the Pendulum Structure

CREEPING VERSUS GALLOPING INFLATION

The preceding litany of costs of inflation alerts us to one very important fact: *predictable inflation is far less burdensome than is unpredictable inflation.* When will an inflation be most predictable? When it proceeds year after year at more or less the same rate. Thus the *variability of the inflation rate* is a crucial factor. Inflation of 9 percent a year for three consecutive years will exact far lower social costs than inflation that is 12 percent in the first year, zero in the second, and 15 percent in the third. In general:

Steady inflation is much more predictable than variable inflation and therefore has much smaller social and economic costs.

But the *average level of the inflation rate* is also important. Partly because of the legal impediments mentioned above and partly because of the more rapid breakdown in normal customer relationships that we have just men-

Contrast and basis of contrast

tioned, a steady inflation of 10 percent a year is more damaging than a steady inflation of 5 percent a year.

Economists distinguish between **creeping inflations** and **galloping inflations** partly on their average level and partly on their variability. Postwar Sweden provided a good example of creeping inflation. During the 13-year period from 1954 to 1967, prices climbed a total of 64 percent (compared with only 24 percent in the United States), for an average annual inflation rate of 3.9 percent. And the pace of inflation was remarkably steady, rarely dropping below 2% percent or rising above 5 percent.

Contrast 1

Germany after World War I suffered through one of the more severe inflations in history. Wholesale prices increased about 80 percent during 1920, over 140 percent in 1921, and a colossal 4100 percent during 1922. At this point, what had been a very impressive galloping inflation simply got out of control. Between December 1922 and November 1923, when a hard-nosed reform finally broke the inflationary spiral, wholesale prices in Germany increased by almost 100 million percent! But even this experience was dwarfed by the great Hungarian inflation of 1945–1946, the greatest inflation of them all. For a period of one year, the rate of inflation averaged about 20,000 percent *per month*. And in the final month (July 1946), the price level skyrocketed 42 quadrillion percent!

Contrast 2

While the distinction between creeping and galloping inflation is a quantitative one, we refrained from putting any specific numbers into the definitions. This is because different societies at different points in time have very different conceptions about what rate constitutes creeping inflation and what rate constitutes galloping inflation. For example, in the United States today, annual rates of inflation in the 6 to 9 percent range are generally considered to be "creeping," while rates in the 25 to 30 percent range would surely be construed as "galloping." In most Latin American countries, however, inflation consistently in the 25 to 30 percent range is viewed as "creeping." And in the United States of the 1950s and early 1960s, a 7 percent annual inflation might have been branded "galloping."

The Costs of Creeping Versus Galloping Inflation

Contrast 3

If you review the costs of inflation that have been enumerated in this chapter, you will see why the distinction between creeping and galloping inflation is so fundamental. Many economists feel we can live very nicely, indeed can prosper, in an environment of creeping inflation. No one feels we can survive very well under galloping inflation.

Under creeping inflation, the rate at which prices rise is relatively easy to predict and to take into account in setting interest rates (as long as the law allows this). Under galloping inflation, where prices are rising at ever-increasing rates, this is very difficult, and perhaps impossible, to accomplish. The potential redistributions become monumental, and as a result, lending and borrowing may cease entirely.

Any inflation makes it difficult to write long-term contracts. With creeping inflation, the "long term" may be 20 years, or 10 years, or 5. But with galloping inflation, the "long term" may be measured in weeks or even hours. Restaurant prices may change before you finish your dessert. Railroad fares may go up while you are in the middle of your journey. When it is impossible to enter into contracts of any duration longer than a few minutes, economic activity becomes paralyzed. We conclude that:

The horrors of galloping inflation either are absent in creeping inflation or are present in such muted forms that they can scarcely be considered horrors.

Creeping Inflation Does Not Necessarily Lead to Galloping Inflation

We noted earlier that inflation is surrounded by a mythology that bears precious little relation to reality. It seems appropriate to conclude this chapter by disposing of one particularly persistent myth: that creeping inflation invariably leads to galloping inflation.

Contrast 4   There is neither statistical evidence nor theoretical support for the myth that creeping inflation leads to galloping inflation. To be sure, creeping inflations sometimes accelerate. But at other times they slow down.

While creeping inflations have many causes, galloping inflations have occurred only when the government has printed incredible amounts of money, usually to finance wartime expenditures.

W. J. Baumol and A. S. Blinder. Economics: Principles and Policy, *2nd Ed., N.Y., Harcourt Brace Jovanovich, 1982, pp. 104–105.*

In the first example, by Woodring, we do not know that a comparison is coming until the parallel is mentioned in the second paragraph. The second example from Baumol and Blinder, clearly indicates a contrast by the introductory word *versus*.

The structural signals occur as in Table 5-1, and again we suggest that when you write your comparison or contrast paper, you should take care to use these terms to clarify what you mean. If you examine the following paragraph, you will see that the contrast is only hinted at after the heading. We do not recommend writing this sort of contrast since it provides no signals after the opening.

Table 5-1   STRUCTURAL SIGNALS
                        COMPARISON – CONTRAST

Comparison—terms of similarity

like	and
as	moreover
similar	in a like fashion
same	in a similar fashion
likewise	comparable to
parallel	conforms to
congruent	

Contrast—terms of difference

unlike	versus (vs.)
different	opposite
dissimilar	by contrast
contrastingly	as a contrast
otherwise	diverging from
however	opposed to
but	differs from
although	is distinguished from

Use vs. Ownership

We can also look at the relation of ownership to actual use of possessions. My interpreter, who spoke English quite well, had been to the Canadian schools, had got some college education, and was therefore wealthy, for in this kind of tribe intelligence correlated very closely with wealth, even in our sense. He was the only man in society who owned an automobile. We were together most of the time, so I could see that he hardly ever used his car. People would come and say, "Teddy how about the key to your car?" And he would pass over the key. As near as I could make out, owning the car for him meant paying for the gas, fixing the tires, coming out and rescuing people in the middle of the reservation who didn't know how to handle it, and so on. The car belonged to anybody who needed it and could ask for it. Obviously the fact that he possessed the only car in the whole society was a point of pride, of pleasure and gratification rather than attracting to him envy, malice, and hostility. The others were glad he had the car and would have been glad if five people had cars instead of just one.

A. H. Maslow. The Farther Reaches of Human Nature, *New York, Viking Press, 1971, p. 197.*

Cause and Effect

If comparison and contrast are the interpretive dimension of classification and definition, cause and effect composition are the interpretive dimensions of narratives and process papers. The emphasis of a cause and effect paper is on *why* a series of events has the order it does.

In the following passage, George Steiner begins with a statement of effect, then quickly goes back in history to a beginning point and traces the three major changes and the reasons behind them, and concludes with a restatement and amplification of the effect. He establishes for the reader that the section is about cause and effect and then gives the causes before he details the effects. He follows a chronological procedure and makes an interpretive narrative:

Problem —
the effect

What brought death to the German language?

Conditions behind
change
the main cause

That is a fascinating and complicated piece of history. It begins with the paradoxical fact that German was most alive before there was a unified German state. The poetic genius of Luther, Goethe, Schiller, Kleist, Heine, and in part that of Nietzsche, pre-dates the establishment of the German nation. The masters of German prose and poetry were men not caught up in the dynamism of Prussian-Germanic national consciousness as it developed after the foundation of modern Germany in 1870. They were, like Goethe, citizens of Europe, living in princely states too petty to solicit the emotions of nationalism. Or, like Heine and Nietzsche, they wrote from outside Germany. And this has remained true of the finest of German literature even in recent times. Kafka wrote in Prague, Rilke in Prague, Paris and Duino.

1st change
an intermediate
cause

The official language of literature of Bismarck's Germany already had in them the elements of dissolution. It is the golden age of the militant historians, of the philologists and the incomprehensible metaphysicians. These mandarins of the new Prussian empire produced that fearful composite of grammatical ingenuity and humorlessness which made the word "Germanic" an equivalent for dead weight. Those who escaped the Prussianizing of the language were the mutineers and the exiles, like those Jews who founded a brilliant journalistic tradition, or Nietzsche, who wrote from abroad.

For to the academicism and ponderousness of German as it was written by the pillars of learning and society between 1870 and the First World War, *the imperial regime added its own gifts of pomp and mystification.* The "Potsdam style" practiced in the chancelleries and bureaucracy of the new empire was a mixture of grossness ('the honest speech of soldiers') and high flights of romantic grandeur (the Wagnerian note). *Thus* university, officialdom, army, and court combined to drill into the German language habits no less dangerous than those they drilled into the German people: a terrible weakness for slogans and pompous clichés. (*Lebensraum*, "the yellow peril," "the Nordic virtues"); an automatic reverence before the long word or the loud voice; a fatal taste for saccharine pathos (Gemütlichkeit) beneath which to conceal any amount of rawness or deception. In this drill, the justly renowned school of *German philology played a curious and complex role.* Philology places words in a context of older or related words, not in that of moral purpose and conduct. It gives to language formality, not form. It cannot be a mere accident that the essentially philological structure of German education yielded such loyal servants to Prussia and the Nazi Reich. The finest record of how the drill call of the

2nd change an intermediate cause

A summary of causes and the general effect

Specific effect Number 1 Specific effects Number 2 Number 3

Third change an additional cause

classroom led to that of the barracks is contained in the novels of Heinrich Mann, particularly in *Der Untertan*.

The final effect

When the soldiers marched off to the 1914 war, so did the words. The surviving soldiers came back, four years later, harrowed and beaten. *In a real sense, the words did not. They remained at the front and built between the German mind and the facts a wall of myth.* They launched the first of those big lies on which so much of modern Germany has been nurtured: the lie of "the stab in the back." The heroic German armies had not been defeated; they had been stabbed in the back by "traitors, degenerates, and Bolsheviks." The Treaty of Versailles was not an awkward attempt by a ravaged Europe to pick up some of the pieces but a scheme of cruel vengeance imposed on Germany by its greedy foes. The responsibility for unleashing war lay with Russia or Austria or the colonial machinations of "perfidious England," not with Prussian Germany.

George Steiner. Language and Silence: Essays on Language, Literature, and the Inhuman, *Atheneum, New York, 1972, pp. 97–98.* (Italics added)

Not all causes nor all effects are historical, but nearly all are related to time, even if very brief periods of time as in the following paragraph about the multiplier effect. Again the author introduces the effect to be explained and the cause.

We can understand how the multiplier works, and see why it is exactly 5 in our model economy, by looking more closely at what actually happens in the economy if businesses decide to spend an additional $1 million on investment goods.

Cause

For the sake of concreteness, suppose that Generous Motors — a major corporation in

Macroland—decides to spend $1 million to retool a factory to manufacture pollution-free electronically powered automobiles. Its $1 million expenditures goes to construction workers and owners of construction companies as wages and profits. That is, it becomes their *income*.

Complication of cause

But the owners and workers of the construction firms will not simply keep their $1 million in the bank. They will spend some of it. If they are "typical" consumers, their spending will, by definition, be $1 million times the marginal propensity to consume (MPC). In our example, the MPC is 0.8. So let us assume that they spend $800,000 and save

Result

the rest. *This $800,000 expenditure is a net addition to the nation's demand for goods and services exactly as GM's original $1 million expenditure was.* So, at this stage, the $1 million investment has already pushed GNP up some $1.8 million.

Result as a cause

But the process by no means stops here. Shopkeepers receive the $800,000 spent by construction workers, and these shopkeepers in turn also spend 80 percent of their new income. This accounts for $640,000 (80 percent of $800,000) in additional consumer spending in the "third round." Next follows a fourth round in which the recipients of the $640,000, in their turn, spend 80 percent of this amount of $512,000, and so on. At each stage in the spending chain, people spend 80 percent of the additional income they receive, and the process continues.

Result

Where does it all end? Does it all end? The answer is that it does, indeed, eventually end—with GNP a total of $5 million higher than it was before Generous Motors spent the original $1 million. The multiplier, as stated, is 5.

Baumol and Blinder, Economics: Principle and Policy, *pp. 178–179.*

Procedure for Determining a Cause or an Effect

When you write a narrative or a process composition, your purpose is generally to set forth the steps or events in order; in a cause and effect composition, however, your purpose is to determine which events or steps are most important in producing a specific result or to determine why a particular order is the way it is. The procedure for making this determination is relatively simple and depends on the three major assumptions most people share.

1. Every action or event has at least one reason, purpose, or motive behind it. There is no such thing as blind chance.
2. Just because two events occur together or in relationship to each other does not mean that one causes the other. Correlation is not causation.
3. There is a difference between asking why something occurred and why something was expected.

The first assumption establishes that there is a principle of cause and effect. The second and third establish a rationale for rejecting some causes and preferring others, first by saying that time sequence or relationship does not make a cause, second by distinguishing between a superficial cause and an underlying principle.

Following these three principles, you might, as a first step, list all the causes you can think of. For instance, if you are writing on the causes of the first World War, you might begin by listing as many events as you can think of:

The assassination of Sarajevo
The arms build-up of the various European nations
The demands for imperial growth
The change in economic power from the landowner to the manufacturer

The espionage incidents
The results of the Boer War
The egotism of the Kaiser
The breaking up of Czarist Russia

The list might be relatively lengthy, and each major event might have several sub-parts. The next task is to group those events. The groupings you might use could be long-term and short-term or economic, political, moral, ideological, and personal. Then you would apply the second and third rules. Does any event seem coincidental, or does it seem to be the result of some third cause that underlies both the event and the outbreak of the war? For example, espionage incidents before the war probably resulted from tension among the countries and were not a cause of the war as much as a part of it. If so, you could reject this item.

Having shortened and classified your list, you can now begin to organize your composition. You might decide on one main cause, or you might give two or more sets of causes and suspend judgement as to which was the main one. Of course, you might also look at the list and decide which cause or causes your reader might accept. You may have to consider these and discuss them.

Whatever choice you make, the major structure of your composition should look something like this:

Thesis statement: name the result and the possible types of causes.
Discuss type one.
Discuss type two.
Conclusion: compare the types.

An alternative arrangement is to accept or reject each type of cause in the paragraph in which you present it, ending up with the most likely cause. In scientific writing the writer often gives several competing reasons or hypotheses and looks for the one that best explains the results. Known as the process of elimination, this structure also dominates many detective stories in which the detective rejects all suspects but one. In the case of causes, however, the issue is usually not innocent or guilty but more probable or less probable.

Generally the writer chooses the causes which best illustrate the subject area for which he or she is preparing the paper. To take the World War I example, a political scientist would probably look at political causes, an historian would concentrate on historical ones, and an economist would examine economic ones. The choice among causes is thus often a choice of perspectives.

The Structure of a Cause-Effect Composition

We have given the general outline of a cause-effect composition. In your own writing of a cause-effect composition you should be clear to signal whether you are moving from cause to effect or effect to cause. The first example gives a cause before an effect.

ENERGY MECHANISMS FOR A WAVE CYCLONE

Cause and effect   The energy for cyclonic circulation comes from the *potential energy* (energy of position) that exists whenever cold and warm air are in juxtaposition, as for example, along a *Cause and process* frontal surface. This potential energy is trans-*described*   ferred into *kinetic energy* (energy of motion) as the air masses involved move in response to density differences. The cold air mass will move under the warmer air so that the discontinuity between them becomes horizontal instead of sloping, as is the case along a front. This means of transferring potential energy into energy of motion might be more easily *Analogy*   visualized if you imagine a tank that has a vertical partition down the middle to separate oil from water. Like air of different densities,

the juxtaposition of these two fluids of different densities provides potential energy.
When the partition separating these fluids is
removed, the water will flow under the less
dense oil until a horizontal surface separates
them. In this way potential energy is trans-

Effect defined in
terms of cause
ferred into motion (kinetic energy). A cyclone
is simply an area where the potential energy
of a dome of cold air is released during sub-
sidence and concentrated as kinetic energy. In
other words, a cyclone is a region of strong
winds.

You might expect that anywhere cold and

Qualification
warm air are in contact, the cold air would
quickly underrun the warm air and thereby
generate winds, but this does not readily
occur because forces other than gravity determine the positions of the air masses involved. The forces that control the movement
of air, in particular the Coriolis force, tend to
hold a mass of cold air in a dome shape, thus
preserving the sloping frontal boundary. It is

Specific determiner
of cause
only when the flow near the front becomes
disturbed that cold air is able to sink and thus
release the energy for cyclonic development.
Once the sinking begins, more and more potential energy is converted into organized cyclonic flow. This energy is available to the
storm until the occlusion process is completed, at which time all of the warm air has
been displaced upward and over the cold air
mass. At that point, without a continued
source of energy, friction quickly brings the
rotating system to a halt.

Frederick K. Lutgens and Edward Tarbuck, The Atmosphere: an
Introduction to Meteorology. *Englewood Cliffs, N.J., Prentice Hall,
1979, p. 206.*

In the following excerpt from a psychology text, the
author gives an effect and then shows how psychologists

reject some causes and suggest others. The organization is close to that of the detective story.

ATTACHMENT

Effect examples

The infant's tendency to seek closeness to particular people and to feel more secure in their presence is called *attachment*. The young of other species show attachment to their mother in different ways. Infant monkeys cling to their mother's chest as she moves about; puppies climb over each other in their attempts to reach the warm belly of their mother; ducklings and baby chicks follow their mother about, making sounds to which she responds and going to her when they are frightened. These early, unlearned responses to the mother have a clear adaptive value: preventing the organism from wandering away from the source of care and getting lost.

Possible cause

Psychologists at first theorized that attachment to the mother developed because she, as a source of food, satisfied one of the infant's most basic needs. But some facts did not fit. For example, ducklings and baby chicks feed themselves from birth, yet they still follow their mothers about and spend a great deal of time in contact with them. The comfort they derive from the mother's presence cannot come from her role in feeding. A series of well-known experiments with monkeys showed that there was more to mother-infant attachment than nutritional needs.

Attachment in Monkeys

Infant monkeys were separated from their mothers shortly after birth and placed with two artificial "mothers" constructed of wire mesh with wooden heads; the torso of one mother was bare wire; the other was covered with foam rubber and terry cloth, making it more cuddly and easy to cling to. ... Either mother could be equipped to provide milk by means of a bottle attached to its chest.

First cause rejected

The experiment sought to determine whether the mother that was always the source of food would be the one to which the young monkey would cling. The results were clear-cut; no matter which mother provided food, the infant monkey spent its time cling-ing to the terry-cloth, cuddly mother. This purely passive but soft-contact mother was a source of security. For example, the obvious fear of the infant monkey placed in a strange environment was allayed if the infant could make contact with the cloth mother. While holding on to the cloth mother with one hand or foot, the monkey was willing to explore objects that were otherwise too terrifying to approach. Similar responses can be observed in 1- to 2-year-old children who are willing to explore strange territory as long as their mother is close by.

Second cause supported

Further studies revealed some additional features that infant monkeys seek in their mothers. They prefer an artificial mother that rocks to an immobile one, and they prefer a warm mother to a cold one. Given a cloth mother and a wire mother of the same tem-perature, the infant monkeys always preferred the cloth mother. But if the wire mother was heated, the newborns chose it over a cool cloth mother for the first two weeks of life. After that, the infant monkeys spent more and more time with the cloth mother.

Cause related to effect

The infant monkey's attachment to its mother is thus an innate response to certain stimuli provided by her. Warmth, rocking, and food are important, but *contact comfort* — the opportunity to cling to and rub against some-thing soft — seems to be the most important attribute for monkeys.

Redefinition of cause

Although contact with a cuddly, artificial mother provides an important aspect of "mothering," it is not enough for satisfactory development. Infant monkeys raised with artificial mothers and isolated from other monkeys during the first six months of life showed various types of bizarre behavior in adulthood. They rarely engaged in normal interaction with other monkeys later on (either cowering in fear or showing abnormally aggressive behavior), and their sexual responses were inappropriate. When female monkeys that had been deprived of early social contact were successfully mated (after considerable effort), they made very poor mothers, tending to neglect or abuse their infants. For monkeys, interaction with other members of their species during the first six months of life appears to be crucial for normal social development.

Atkinson, Atkinson, and Hilgard. Introduction to Psychology, *New York, Harcourt Brace Jovanovich, p. 75.*

The verbal clues in both examples are relatively straightforward and clearly signaled. Both use words like "theorized" and "because" and both follow a chronological sequence. Other signal words and phrases are listed in Table 5-2.

Writing to Develop a Thesis

So far in this chapter we have explored two kinds of interpretive writing that are fairly clear in their ends and their structures. You will find however, that often the assignment you will receive may be less specific than those we have discussed, an assignment like:

Discuss China's relations with the United States from World War II to the ouster of Chiang Kai-Shek.

Table 5-2   TERMS INDICATING CAUSE AND EFFECT

Cause

reason	how it happens that
cause	stem from
why	begin with
rationale	come from
how	plays a role in
behind	underlie
because	account for
for the reason that	lie behind

Effect

effect	turns out
result	proceeds from
end	that is how
thus	come about
so	shows that
results in	as a result
grows out of	it follows
ends up as	

Write a critical discussion of color imagery in *Macbeth*.
Write a paper analyzing the role of language patterning
    in human development.

This kind of assignment leaves it up to you to create or
discover a problem in the topic, come up with a thesis, and
determine the particular kind of structure you should use to
discuss that thesis. A good part of academic writing is defining the issue in a topic and then turning the issue into a
thesis you can support.

The steps you need to go through include turning a
topic into a thesis, providing a means of proving that thesis,
and discussing the results of your attempts to prove it. A
thesis is an educated guess about some phenomenon. It
may ask questions, as the following introduction to a book
on philosophy does:

Area defined   Criticism is a form of studied discourse about
                        works of art. It is a use of language primarily
                        designed to facilitate and enrich the under-

standing of art. Involved in its practice are highly developed sets of vocabularies, various sorts of procedures and arguments, broad assumptions, and a vast diversity of specific goals and purposes.

These assumptions, procedures, terms, and goals are perennially scrutinized by critics and by those philosophers who are interested in criticism as one area of aesthetic inquiry. Certain problems have come to be recognized as basic in the philosophy of criticism. Among them are: the meaning and legitimacy of the fundamental terms of criticism; the validation of critical utterance; the nature of critical disagreement; the nature of critical argument; and the primary function of criticism. Is criticism objective or subjective? Is it verifiable or mere expression of feeling? Are there absolute standards of evaluation? Is criticism important or trivial in the understanding of art? These are but some of the specific questions raised by critics or philosophers in the traditional philosophy of criticism. In criticism itself, whole schools have arisen and still arise giving large-scale answers to these particular questions and to the central question of the exact nature of criticism. Critics call themselves — but more often call their opponents — "impressionistic," "historical," "psychological," "biographical," "stylistic," and even "new," thinking that labels characterize and distinguish their answers to the question: What is criticism?

Question raised

Although philosophers may probe more deeply than critics these questions of objectivity, meaning, argument, and validation, however vague philosophers realize these questions are, they concur for the most part with the critics in this omnibus approach to the philosophy of criticism. What is criticism? is, for them, as central and clear a question as it is for the critics themselves.

I agree with the critics and philosophers

that these traditional questions about the objectivity, meaning, justification, and function of critical utterance are important in the philosophy of criticism. But I cannot accept the persistent logical motivation of traditional philosophy of criticism that a definitive and univocal answer is forthcoming in the question, What is criticism? For, if we actually "look and see" (to borrow a phrase from Wittgenstein), i.e., if we examine what critics do in their essays of criticism instead of what they *say* they do in their philosophical moments or what philosophers sometimes say critics do or must do, we will uncover answers to what criticism is that are radically different from the traditional ones in the philosophy of criticism. Indeed, thinking about this discrepancy between what critics do when they criticize and what they or others say they do has led me to the writing of this book.

*Approach
to be used*

*Hypothesis
generated*

Morris Weitz. Hamlet and the Philosophy of Literary Criticism, *Chicago & London, The University of Chicago Press, 1964, pp. vii – viii.*

As you can see, the writer has chosen the topic of criticism (as if the assignment were "Discuss criticism"), has turned the topic into a question, has looked at the question from two perspectives (what do critics say? what do they do?), and from this process has generated a thesis: A discrepancy exists between what critics say they do and what they actually do. This thesis leads the writer to follow a lengthy exercise in comparison contrast in the rest of the book.

The first step in developing a thesis, then, is to turn an area into a question. Question or problem finding is not easy, and we do not have any magic formula to help you. We do have, however, some criteria by which you may judge questions. To take an example from English literature, suppose you were asked to write a critical paper on the following poem:

ANIMAL TRANQUILLITY AND DECAY

The little hedgerow birds,
That peck along the road, regard him not.
He travels on, and in his face, his step,
His gait, is one expression: every limb,
His look and bending figure, all bespeak
A man who does not move with pain, but
    moves
With thought. — He is insensibly subdued
To settled quiet: he is one by whom
All effort seems forgotten; one to whom
Long patience hath such mild composure
    given,
That patience now doth seem a thing of which
He hath no need. He is by nature led
To peace so perfect that the young behold
With envy, what the Old Man hardly feels.
             William Wordsworth

As you prepare your discussion, you need to find a question that you can then transform into your thesis statement. Three criteria will help you select a question leading to your thesis.

1. "Is it a real question?" That is to say, is the question one that seems to have a number of possible answers, not a question that can be answered simply by a yes or no or by a fact? Some questions that might occur are "Who is the old man?" "Why is he the way he is?" "Where is the story in this poem?" "Is this all?" "What does the poet mean by the title?" "How does the poem build up to the last line?" "Is it a good poem?" The first four questions are probably not real questions for the purposes of discussing the poem. The answer to the first two are, "we don't know," and to the third and fourth, "there is no story"—that is all. The other four questions either singly or perhaps combined might make a good question for a composition.

2. "Can you defend the answer to the question, or is it simply a matter of opinion?" A *yes* answer to the second half of the question will probably not produce a good composition. You can answer "Is it a good poem?" with "Yes, I like it," and no one can refute or even discuss your answer. You need to rework the question into an arguable form that leads to an hypothesis such as "Wordsworth has created a successful portrait without physically describing the person portrayed." The hypothesis contains a paradox which your paper can explore.

3. Can I answer the question I have with the information, space, or time I have? A question like "Why did Wordsworth write this poem?" is a perfectly good question, real and possibly arguable, but you may not have the time or the resources to answer it.

Once you have selected the question, you need to turn the question into a thesis statement. The subject of the thesis sentence should be "Animal Tranquillity and Decay." The predicate will be your comment on the subject: "portrays a man without describing him." The whole thesis statement, then, is: *"Animal Tranquillity and Decay" portrays a man without describing him.* In many cases the course you are writing for will determine the kind of predicate you choose, but occasionally you will make that choice as well as the choice of the specific predicate.

In the following example, the major portion of an article on Indonesian kinship, the writer has turned the subject, kinship, into a question: When societies become urban, are traditional kinship patterns lost? From this question has emerged the thesis: A simple notion of the loss of traditional kinship when modernization comes [Subject → Comment] must be seen as an inadequate generalization. It is the predicate that turns the subject into a thesis that he can develop. He develops it using a variety of techniques.

Over a century ago Sir Henry Maine told us that kinship, the basis of primitive and social organization, declines in importance in more advanced societies. The proposition has been widely accepted and has been restated in one form or another by many scholars during the last hundred years. Most recently, for example, Julian Steward (1960) writes that internal specialization, social classes, and state institutions come to supersede kinship groups, and Leslie White (1959, p. 141) goes so far as to suggest that the transformation from primitive to civil society entails "the loss of kinship."

Criticisms have been made of Sir Henry's proposition on the grounds that not only kinship but also territorial groups and age-sex groupings are significant in the social life of many primitive peoples, and on the grounds that kinship often plays a crucial role in some urban social systems. These points are well taken; nevertheless if we take the long view, and especially at extreme ends of the developmental continuum, Sir Henry's generalization appears to be essentially correct. It is perfectly clear that kinship was more prominent among Australian aborigines of the last century than it is today in urban centers of the Western nations.

The generalization is less clear, however, if we focus on intermediate level societies, those that are neither truly primitive nor fully urbanized, or if we focus on societies that have recently been exposed to modernizing influences and are currently undergoing rapid culture change. In many of these societies even a preliminary analysis of the role of kinship takes us far beyond the confines of Sir Henry's proposition. I agree with Oscar Lewis (1962) that the distinction between kinship-based versus nonkinship-based societies simply does not tell us enough for purposes of comparative analysis. We now have field studies of the processes of

Failures in the generalization

kinship change and of the details of the sequence in which change occurs, and on the basis of these data we must formulate theoretical distinctions finer than those proposed by Sir Henry. His generalization and other similar evolutionary propositions were and are important advances, but rather than repeat or defend them, we must aim for more sophisticated formulations which take account of the more complete data now being fathered by anthropologists from a wider range of societies.

Limits of argument and thesis referring to a specific instance

This brief paper is more limited in scope. It explores the role of kinship among the Toba Batak located in the modern coastal city of Medan, Indonesia; demonstrates the inadequacy of broad statements to the effect that kinship declines in importance, is superseded, or even "lost" in urban societies; and presents some tentative conclusions which may be applicable in other similar situations. [The author provides several paragraphs of background on the people and the city.]

Summary of background and basis for supporting thesis

The urban migrant finds himself in a radically different physical and social environment. The rural villages are approximately 3,000 feet above sea level and hence are considerably cooler than the coastal city. The villages lack electricity, running water, telephone service, and paved streets, while the city has all of these and more, including restaurants, hotels, hospitals, department stores, banks, theaters, publishing houses, daily newspapers, universities, a medical school, and other facilities normally associated with a busy metropolitan center and regional capital. The language spoken in the village is Toba Batak, while in the city it is Indonesian; the two are mutually unintelligible. Almost all village men, even those who are teachers or government employees, are at least part-time farmers, and village women regularly work in the fields along with their husbands. Most

101

urban men work in an office and neither they nor their wives engage in any agricultural activity. But possibly the most significant difference is that in the village everyone is not only a Toba Batak but also a close relative, while in the city one's immediate neighbors are most likely to be strangers.

In sum, Medan is a relatively new city, characterized by a constant influx of migrants, by rapid growth, high poulation density, ethnic diversity, and cultural heterogeneity. The Batak migrant leaves his familiar village world or kinsmen to settle among strangers in an alien environment. It is in this context that we inquire into the role of kinship in the city.

Introduction of support

The Role of Kinship

Evidence to support thesis

The Toba Batak residing in Medan are part of a single kinship community, in that every person is bound by multiple ties in a widely ramifying kinship network. The urban Batak are very aware of their relationships to kinsmen; they employ kinship terminology in daily life, and the kinship system is symbolized at all life-crisis rites and ceremonials.

Kinship ties are based on both descent and marriage. Let us consider each in turn. The Batak descent system is a patrilineal one which operates on many levels of segmentation. At the highest level the Toba Batak form a single super-patrilineage, since they consider themselves to be descendants of one man, Si Radja Batak, who existed, they say, about 25 generations ago. Below the super-patrilineage are groupings of clans, named exogamous clans, maximal and minimal lineages. Every Batak, living and dead, has a place on the tribal genealogy and persons in different descent lines are always able to determine their proper relationship to one another by tracing their social distance from a common male ancestor. In addition to the descent system, relationships are also reckoned through affinal ties, as every Batak marriage binds two or more lineages or clans. When a man is married, not only he, but every member of his descent group immediately becomes related to all members of the bride's lineage. These affinal bonds are always significant in social life as they involve a status relationship, ceremonial obligations, and the exchange of money, goods, and services. They may be further reinforced by additional marriages in subsequent generations, thus creating affinal alliances which have structural continuity over time. Every descent group, at any given time, has a series of affinal alliances or more transitory ties to those lineages to whom they have given wives and to those from whom they have received wives. Thus in Batak society there is a kind of kinship grid binding all individuals vertically through descent lines and horizontally through affinal bonds.

[There follow several paragraphs of additional supporting evidence.]

Conclusion of support of particular evidence and summary of findings

The aim of this paper has been to examine the extent to which kinship has declined in importance in an urban environment, and we are primarily interested in drawing conclusions about the direction of change. Thus we need a base line for purposes of comparison. Rather than compare the contemporary urban system with a reconstructed "aboriginal system" floating in a hypothetical "ethnographic present," the reference point for each statement about the changing role of kinship in the city will be the contemporary village system. My data support the following series of propositions:

1. The urban Batak form a single kinship community, and the sense of ethnic identity is stronger among Toba Batak in

the city than in the village.

2. The range of the kinship system has been extended more widely in the city to encompass a larger number of more distantly related persons.

3. Social relationships among urban kinsmen are generally less personal, intimate, and familial than in the village.

4. The minimal lineage, which includes some members who reside in the village and others who live in the city, continues to be a meaningful, cooperative, corporate group.

5. The urban Batak form clan associations, a corporate unit intermediate in size between the lineage and the community, which serve many social and ceremonial functions not performed by the village clan system.

6. The nuclear family is more important in the city than in the village.

[There follow a few paragraphs leading back to the main issue and generalization.]

Reference to subject to be refuted

Indications of kinship breakdown should be more readily apparent among those segments of the urban community who occupy higher positions in the stratification system. Those who are wealthy, better educated, and who have lived in Medan the longest should have changed the most. A traditional, poorly educated, recent migrant is, in effect, a transplanted villager. The urban Batak community is stratified, but rather than study the differences between various groupings within the city, I was primarily concerned with a rural-urban comparison. In order to differentiate more clearly between village and city, I focused upon the wealthy elite and the upper classes of Medan; my aim was to contrast extremes. Thus the data on the urban system were gathered from among those who were the most modern and upwardly mobile in the city. If extended kin ties were in process of breakdown, I should have found it within this social segment; the fact that I did not lends further support to my position.

Questions about validity of thesis

Nevertheless, the generalizations of the evolutionists may prove to be valid in the long run; possibly I have simply described one stage in the urbanization process. If this is so, then I am not entirely sure how long one has to wait for the process to complete itself: the customary one or two generations, or perhaps one or two centuries, or even longer. It is my feeling, however, that the creative adaptation to the city made by the Batak of Medan is neither unique nor transitory. The

Reaffirmation of thesis

Batak clan groups bear some similarity to the clan associations of the overseas Chinese, to the urban tribal association of West Africa, and to the *zaibatsu* of industrial Japan. I suspect that future research on changing kinship systems among societies of the middle range now undergoing rapid cultural change, and among the newly urbanized peoples of Asia and Africa, will disclose not only the maintenance of existing kinship ties, but also the development of novel and stable recombinations based upon traditional structural principles.

Edward M. Bruner. "Medan: The Role of Kinship in an Indonesian City." A. Spoehr ed. Pacific Port Towns and Cities, A Symposium Honolulu, Bishop Museum Press, 1963, pp. 1–12.

The Structure of Thesis Papers

The organization of a thesis paper is relatively straightforward. Most of the work has been done in shaping the question and moving from question to thesis. All that is left is several hours or days slogging to fill in the blanks.

> Statement of the thesis
> Justification of the perspective
> Assembly of the evidence
> Conclusion: The thesis is confirmed or denied.

In general, except for the construction *if-then* and a set of terms giving the *pro* argument for your answer and the *con* argument for your opponents, most of the signalling words and phrases refer to narrative or process, description, classification, definition, cause-effect, or comparison-contrast. We repeat the table that appeared in Chapter 2, adding pros and cons. (Table 5-3)

A good illustration of the structure of a thesis paper can be seen in the following section of a book on information theory.

Subject announced	The "arrow of time" is a metaphor invented by Sir Arthur Eddington to express the idea that there exists a purely physical distinction between past and future, independent of consciousness. Such a distinction is based on the entropy principle, which asserts that as time goes on energy tends to be transformed from
Basis of subject	an orderly into a less orderly form. In Eddington's view, earlier is different from later because earlier energy is more highly orga-
Repetition of basis and reasons for acceptance	nized. There is no need to appeal to our intellectual sense of the passing of time to explain why *now* is not the same as *then*. It is
Support (if-then)	all a question of degree of organization. If there is more and more randomness along the path of the arrow, it points toward the future. If there is less and less randomness, it
Contrast (unlike)	points toward the past. Unlike space, which has no preferred direction, time is asymmetrical, always moving forward, never backward, and it behaves in this fashion whether human beings are there to experience it or not. Time's arrow is irreversible, because entropy cannot decrease of its own accord

Table 5-3   TYPICAL ORGANIZATIONS
OF DISCOURSE

ORGANIZED BY TIME

Narration: Chronological development. May be rearranged with flashbacks
or may have two or more simultaneous series of events.

Process: Chronological or step–by–step development. May include a list of
parts or ingredients.

Typical signals:

once	first	second	later	and
next	after	before	then	

Cause–effect: Like process but may go from effect to cause or cause
to effect.

Typical signalling words:

the reason for	consequently	therefore	by means of	thus
result from	and so	because	effect	

ORGANIZED BY SPACE

Descriptive: Develops by a geometrical or geographical arrangement—
usually horizontal, vertical, or circular. May follow a map or a
topographical arrangement.

Typical signals:

besides	below	down from	as we move	around
above	in front of	near	as you go	about
next to	behind	following	proceeding	

ORGANIZED BY COMMON LOGIC

Classificatory: Develops by dividing object or event into parts and
explaining relationships or difference of parts.

Definitive: Develops by giving distinctions of the object or event from others
similar to it.

Typical signals:

to constitute	to limit to	let us define	may be divided
progressive	succession	as follows	into
is called	is seen as	a), b), c)	is made up of
: (colon)			1), 2), 3)

Comparison–contrast: Organized by relating or differentiating two or more
objects or events.

Typical signals:

may be distinguished from	compared to	as	but
differs from	distinct from	on the other hand	

PROS AND CONS

Pro:	Con:
strongly support	against
in fact	fail to
indeed	do not consider
truly	deny
unquestionable	fail to support

without violating the second law of thermodynamics. A reversible arrow would be like a movie run backward. The scenes in the movie are not impossible by the laws of classical mechanics, but they are patently absurd. Only the one-wayness of physical time, from more to less organization, Eddington said, insures that the world makes sense.

Con (common sense objection)

However, ordinary common sense tells us that something is wrong here. If time's arrow follows the path of increasing randomness, it wipes out information. Yet history is not a record of things unraveling, descending into chaos, but of new types of order and a richer store of information. As it moves through centuries and millennia, history is a chronicle of novelty — new structures, new organisms, new civilizations, new ideas. Information, which is a measure of novelty, increases rather than diminishes with the passage of the years.

Con-alternative position

David Layzer, a Harvard astronomer, has recently presented a theory which suggests a universe starting from simplicity, but growing more complex and richer in information as time goes on. At each successive moment of its history, there is something in it that is entirely new. Here Layzer is speaking, not just about the planet earth, with its wealth of living forms, but about the cosmos as a whole.

Con-contradiction of two positions

There is certainly a paradox here if, as Eddington claims, the arrow of time is supposed to point in the direction of increasing entropy and disorder. For, as new and highly detailed accounts of the birth of the universe, split second by split second, show, time might just as well be said to flow in the direction of greater order and complexity. A second paradox arises from the fact that underneath the surface of matter, in the microcosm of particles and forces, the fundamental processes of physics, with one very minor exception, are reversible. The backward-running movie may be nonsensical, but the events it portrays do not violate these microscopic physical laws, which are very nearly time-symmetric. They breach only the statistical, "fact-like" assumptions that follow from the entropy principle.

Resolution of contradiction and introduction of thesis: three complementary views

Layzer looks for a way out of these paradoxes by proposing not one, but three arrows of time. One of these is the arrow of cosmic expansion, pointing away from the initial state of the universe, a state which was infinitely condensed and uniform. The second is the arrow of history, defined by all the rich, evolving structures of galaxies, stars, planets, life, civilization, and mind. The third is the thermodynamic arrow, the arrow of increasing entropy, which is generated by the unraveling or macroscopic structures.

Second view

In Layzer's theory, the arrow of history points irreversibly in the direction of increasing complexity, increasing information. Un-

Contrast with other views

like some contemporary astronomers, Layzer does not believe that the universe began in a state of disequilibrium and is running down into a state of equilibrium, or maximum entropy. In his view, there was no need for the universe, at its birth, to have any structure whatever. If the big-bang theory of cosmic genesis is correct, the universe could have started out totally devoid of information, both on the very small scale of its microscopic particles and on the large, macroscopic scale of its visible appearance. Uniform disorder prevailed at the beginning. Information, regarded as a measure of the nonuniform, orderly properties of physical systems, evolved out of that initial state of perfect confusion.

Cause and effect: return to first view

Cosmic expansion was the reason why the infant universe departed from a state of maximum entropy. As long as the processes which randomized the distribution of energy and the concentrations of various types of particles were very fast, faster than the rate at which the cosmos was expanding, equilibrium could be maintained. Bits of atoms smashed into one another in the confusion of that very dense undifferentiated state with such frequency that no structures could arise. But this state of affairs lasted only for a brief fraction of a microsecond. The speed of the cosmic expansion was not constant, and once it became greater than the speed at which the forces of disorder could degrade information by collisions, chemical equilibrium was broken. As encounters between particles became less frequent, due to the greater distances between them, the equal distribution of different kinds of particles could not be maintained.

Result and reference to third view

Thus the chemical composition of the universe changed from a state of equilibrium to one of disequilibrium as the expansion proceeded, and this change was to have momentous consequences. For it is the chemical disequilibrium of the sun that is the source of free energy on which all life on earth depends. If the cosmos had expanded at a slower speed than was in fact the case, all the matter in it would have become pure ash, as if a coal fire burned away every scrap of its fuel with complete efficiency. However, because the forces of equilibrium did not keep pace with the expansion, the universe could not consume all its fuel, thereby enabling long-burning stars like our own sun to evolve, and ultimately the kingdoms of animal and vegetable life. So the cosmic expansion created a set of initial conditions that made possible two quite different kinds of order-generating processes: cosmic evolution and

Third view

biological evolution. The direction of this latter process is also irreversibly away from the uniformity and toward new forms of structure and greater complexity. It traces a path in time

Comparison of views and reconciliation

that is described by the arrow of history. Along this path, too, points the thermodynamic arrow, because entropy arises naturally as a result of the very processes which give rise to living systems and drive the engine of human civilization, with its increasing dependence on the energy-degrading machines of modern technology. But the arrow of history and the thermodynamic arrow are complementary, not in conflict. One is not more natural or more fundamental than the other. The view Layzer challenges is the one that says the growth of entropy is a necessary feature of the world, while the growth of order is somehow an accident. This is not the case. Both follow logically from events which took place at the first instant after the big bang.

Jeremy Campbell. Grammatical Man: Information, Entropy, Language, and Life, *New York: Simon and Schuster, 1982, pp. 84 – 86.*

In this description of a scientific theory, the writer has followed the outline of a thesis paper exactly; he stops here, and moves on to a further ramification. In fact, the whole book explores a thesis about the relationship of physics, information theory, genetic coding, and language. In the course of expounding this argument, the author has combined the pro-con, cause-effect, and comparison-contrast. Most writers use a number of organizational methods to support their interpretations. You can use all the evidence and as many types of argument as you wish.

HOW TO PUT GRAMMAR TO WORK FOR YOU TO MAKE YOUR WRITING CLEAR

6

You have probably studied English grammar many times before, so we are not going to review all of the rules of grammar and usage in this chapter, nor are we going to present a whole grammatical system. Instead we are going to present a number of grammatical points which we think will help you make your writing clearer to your reader.

One of the problems you may have had with grammar is that you weren't quite sure why you were studying it. Why did you have to name parts of speech and draw diagrams? The important question though is "What good is grammar and what is the grammar good for?"

What is the role of the grammar? How can knowing about grammar help you? One answer is that it helps sometimes to make language the object of conscious analysis, to try to gain distance from something that is part of your daily life and activities so that you become more conscious of its possibilities and of its limitations. Grammar's relation to writing is something like physics' relation to golf; knowing helps you understand what you are doing, but it will not automatically improve your score. At its best, knowing the grammar helps you become more aware of how language works, because grammar makes something known explicitly that you often may have only felt implicitly. Our attempt to make you conscious of language cannot and need not be in any way exhaustive. Some of the basic principles are enough.

You need to be aware of the relationships between:

a) forms of language and functions of language (and that there is no one-to-one relationship: one form can have many functions and several different forms can serve a general function, such as the various ways of persuading someone to do something;

b) forms of language and notional categories (such as the verb tense system and the expression of time relations).

After a brief review of these two sets of relationships, we will discuss two ways of using grammar to make your writing clear:

1. How to show connections between ideas and sentences, and

2. How to use verb tenses to show relationships between events and to get your point across.

The Forms of Language and the Functions of Language

If you write using a conscious knowledge of grammar and certain functions of language, such as those we outlined in

Table 1-1, you can use language to *affect* your readers. In the following list, we indicate some of these functions. You can use a grammatical form to help you make your point just as well as a special word or phrase. In some cases such as persuading or requesting functions, you can use alternative forms to nudge your reader. They are more subtle than direct forms.

Functions	*Grammatical Forms*
A. Persuasion	
1. Direct	1. Imperatives Go to see *Raiders of the Lost Ark!*
2. Indirect	2. Statements or questions: Everyone should see *Raiders of the Lost Ark.* How about seeing *Raiders of the Lost Ark?* *Raiders of the Lost Ark* is playing. (This is an indirect invitation.)

Each of these might end a review. You have a grammatical choice as to how directive you want to be.

B. Request for information	
1. Direct	1. Questions/interrogative sentences: Do you know anything about it?
2. Indirect	2. Statements: I wonder if anyone knows anything about it.

In a composition, of course, you don't use this sort of request to get information but to move your reader along. To a teacher, the indirect request is less belligerent.

C. Request for action

1. Direct	1. Question: Would you look at Table 1, please?
2. Indirect	2. Statements: If you look at Table 1, ... Table 1 will show you . . . . As Table 1 proves . . . . The information in Table 1 needs to be noted carefully before . . . .

Perhaps one of the most important relations between grammatical form and function is in the English verb system. Although the verb system has only a few tenses, if you consider just one, such as the simple present, you can see that it expresses many concepts and performs many functions.

Forms	*Concepts*	*Functions*
A. Simple present tense in active, affirmative, de-clarative sentences		
1. It *gets* dark when the sun goes down.	Permanent truth or situation	Giving information
2. I *am* tired today. I *have* $20 in my bank account.	Less permanent state or situation (particularly be and have)	Giving information/indirect refusal of invitation, etc. depending on the context of situation
3. Dan *kicks* the ball to John.	Quick, finished event	Giving information/reporting

4. Slowly the President's car *approaches* the bridge.	Expected/predictable event is taking place	Giving information/reporting
5. We *leave* tomorrow.	Future event which takes place in accordance with a plan or schedule	Giving information/overcoming objections/refusing suggestions, etc. depending on the context

Notice that although the passive voice in English has some useful functions, you should generally avoid using it except in special cases.

Passive forms	*Concepts*	*Functions*
1. The window *is broken*.	State/indefinite agent	Giving information when the agent is unknown or unimportant

The alternative—*Someone or something broke the window*—is awkward.

2. The experimental rats were weighed and were given the 4cc saline solution and allowed to rest for an hour. Then they were put in a maze with sixteen turns and timed. They were then weighed a second time, allowed to rest	Sequence of events/indefinite agent	Giving information, describing, reporting/focus on subject

another hour, put
back in the maze,
and weighed
again. Five of the
six lost weight.

When you must focus on one person or thing to illustrate a process, your sentences will flow easily if you use the passive. In the example, who did what to the rats is unimportant: And so the sentence focuses on the procedure. If only one person had performed the experiment, you could write the passage in the active voice —*I weighed* the *rats, injected them with 4cc,* etc. — but this way of writing shifts the focus away from the rats to the experimenter.

3. Your *request has been turned down*.	Event/indefinite agent	Giving information/hiding behind an anonymous decision-making procedure/expressing regret, approval, etc. depending on context.

This form may work in some situations, but you should avoid it in academic writing.

Many teachers object to the passive voice because it can lead to imprecise, irresponsible writing. You should always ask yourself whether your use of the passive voice is absolutely necessary to your meaning.

A Summary of Some Grammatical Forms and How They Illustrate Certain Notions

Much grammar helps to indicate relationships among words, not as an abstract system, but as words that represent what you think and feel, what you want to write about. The following list recaps some of the functions of grammar to indicate various conceptual relationships between such ideas and feelings, which we have discussed earlier in this book as narrative and process, cause and effect, or spatial relationships.

Concepts	*Grammatical Forms*
A. *Time relations*	
1. To indicate the general order of events — when things happen	1. <u>Tense system of the verbs:</u> Smith *was born*, Smith *lives*, Smith *will die*.
2. To indicate the frequency of events — how often things happen	2. a) <u>Verbs:</u> e.g., present tense/habitual I *wake up* at six.
	b) <u>Adverbs:</u> *never, sometimes, often*
	c) <u>Adverbial constructions:</u> *on Tuesdays, every week, daily*
3. To indicate a specific point of time — precisely when things happen	3. a) <u>Adverbs:</u> *yesterday, tomorrow*
	b) <u>Adverbial constructions:</u> *at six, this evening,* June 1, 1776, on the following day
4. To indicate dura-tion — how long things go on happening	4. a) <u>Ing-form of the verb:</u> He *is talking* (*has been talking*) a long time on the phone.
	b) <u>Adverbial constructions:</u> I've lived here *since* 1980.

I'll stay here *for two weeks.*

B. To indicate a continued *reference* to something or somebody (For a fuller discussion see the next section of this chapter)

1. <u>Personal pronouns:</u> Churchill was in Parliament. *He* had two children.

2. <u>Articles + nouns:</u> *The man's* daughter was an actress.

3. <u>Demonstrative pronouns:</u> this, that, these, those *This* career was a surprise.

4. <u>Relative pronouns:</u> Particularly to those *who* were snobs.

5. <u>Other demonstratives:</u> *here*, there Here we have a transition in attitudes.

6. <u>Temporal modifiers:</u> now, then *Now*, no one would care.

C. To indicate *cause* and *result*, a topic you will deal with frequently. You can use conjunctions that join clauses, prepositional phrases that contain cause and effect in one clause, verbs that show cause, adverbs that show the relationships between clauses or sentences, indirect expressions, and, of course, a noun phrase

1. <u>Conjunctions:</u>
   a. because
      We arrived late *because* the weather was so bad.
   b. so . . . that
      It had rained *so* much *that* the river flooded.
   c. as, since
      Since it was already too late, we decided to stay at home.

2. <u>Prepositional phrases:</u> because of, on account of We were late *because of* the bad weather.

119

3. <u>Verbs:</u>
   a. cause, lead to, result in, give rise to
      The bad weather *caused* us to be late.
   b. make
      His behavior *made* me angry.
   c. result from, be the result of
      Our failure *resulted from* our negligence.

D. The *roles* that people, things or ideas play in the world are many, but English (unlike other languages) has only a limited number of grammatical forms or positions for nouns, pronouns, or noun phrases. These forms are called cases, and in English the three cases are the *subject* of a verb, the *object* either of a verb or a preposition, and the *indirect object* of a verb. Nevertheless these three grammatical cases can indicate a variety of roles to show the writer's meaning.
   1. The *actor*, or who or what is doing the action in a sentence, is usually the grammatical subject.

      You sing very well.
      The rats entered the maze.

   2. The *object* of the action is usually the grammatical object.

      John opened *the letter*.

3. The person, thing or idea *affected* by the action in a sentence can be the indirect object, but also the object, or the subject.

I gave the money *to her*.
John told *Jane* a dirty joke.
I was struck by a falling branch.
He believed he was right.
[In terms of meaning the belief affects the person.]

4. The *instrument* or means by which an action is carried out can be the subject or an adverbial.

The key opened the door.
The burglar opened the door *with a key*.

5. The *location* in space or time of an action can be the subject or an adverbial.

Urbana is a windy city.
April is the cruelest month.
You'll find it *in the drawer*.
We'll go *on Saturday*.

6. The *result* of an action in a sentence can be the object, but in some cases it can be the subject, particularly if the action refers to a process.

Mother is baking *a cake*.
The cake is baking in the oven.
[It isn't a cake until after it is taken out.]

7. The *beneficiary* of an action in a sentence can be the subject or an indirect object.

I got a nice birthday present.
I changed the ticket *for her*.

We realize that we have given you only a short summary of what is called "Case Grammar," a grammar which seeks to relate the forms of language to the meaning the writer intends. If you want to read more about this approach to grammar, we recommend: Fillmore, Charles. "The Case for Case." In *Universals in Linguistic Theory*, edited by E. Bach and R. T. Harms. New York: Holt, 1968.

We hope that this section on grammar has suggested to you that grammar has a very important part to play in using language. Once you realize you can use different language structures to express various functions and concepts, not only can you observe what the *typical* relationships between functions, concepts, and forms are but also the *range* of all possible connections. We believe that such conscious attention to the focus of language will help you become more aware of the different possibilities you have to use language. Although later you may pay less conscious attention to grammar matters, at first you will need to concentrate on perfecting your skills.

One of the advantages of a conscious effort to examine alternative ways to write something is that you will vary your constructions and will avoid fossilizing some patterns. Experiment with your writing to make sure that the grammar you use helps you to say what you mean. Take the role of the reader to see if the literal meaning of what you have written matches your intentions as the writer.

Using Grammar to Connect Your Thoughts

In our various charts of connectors we have only briefly mentioned the most frequent kind because you probably use them correctly without thinking about them. These connectors, of course, are *repetitions* and *pronouns*. Many studies have shown that clear writing repeats verbs but, more particularly, nouns from sentence to sentence — either the same noun and verb or synonyms for them. Clear writing also uses pronouns like *it, they, them, we, you* or demonstratives like *this* and *that* to connect ideas within and across sentences. These connectives show the reader the relationship between sentences or paragraphs. But such connectives do not show the nature of that relationship. The words in the Tables in Chapters 4 and 5 (pages 52, 59, 68–69, 83, 95) are the ones that show *how* the idea and events in sentences and paragraphs are connected.

Some types of words, especially demonstratives and pronouns, often refer back to something already named. This connection is called *Anaphoric Reference*.

Example:
Peter said he wouldn't be here until about 3 o'clock.

In this sentence the word "he" refers back to "Peter." In the same way a word or a phrase can refer forward to something the author is about to explain. This is called *Cataphoric Reference*.

Example:
Here is the news. Early today a bomb exploded in . . .

In this sentence "here" refers to the actual elements of news which follow.

For practice pick out all the examples of anaphora and cataphora in one of your compositions, and then circle the anaphoric/cataphoric word and the reference and join them with an arrow running to the reference. If you can't find a target for your arrow, you have a problem. We have provided you with an example in the Exercise section, p. 76.

Anaphora

    A. Specific Antecedent
        1. Use of pronouns (The impersonal use of they, we, you, one, and it usually has no reference except a vague one. "*We* have already shown that . . ." refers not to a person but to one or two paragraphs.)
        2. This, that, these, those
    B. Broader Antecedent
        1. Impersonal personal pronouns (we, one, it, they)
        2. This, that, these, those
        3. The preceding, the foregoing, as above
        4. What (as in phrases "What I have said . . .")

Cataphora

    A. Specific indicators of what follows
       1. This, these
       2. There in "There is . . ."
    B. Broader indicators of what follows
       1. As follows, the following, here is, thus

Verbs as Connectors and Indicators of Time

Writers use verbs, particularly the tenses of verbs, to indicate sequence in narrative and process papers. You may have heard you should generally use consistent tenses: "Stay in the past," or "Use the present." But if you look closely at academic writing, you will find that this generalization doesn't hold up. There are both logic and a set of conventions about using verb tenses in academic composition. If you look again at the following selection from a history text on the election of 1860 you will notice that the writers did not stick to one time or one tense.

past	The election of 1860, judged by its consequences, was the most momentous in American history.
past	As the Democrats gathered in convention in Charleston, South Carolina, in April most of the Southern delegates came with the determination to adopt a platform providing for federal protection of slavery in the territories:
present (a definition)	that is an official endorsement of the principles of the Dred Scott decision. The Western
present	Democrats, arriving with bitter recollections
past perfect (prior time)	of how Southern influence had blocked their legislative demands in the recent Congress,
past	were angered at the rule-or-ruin attitude of
past	the Southerners. The Westerners hoped, however, to negotiate a face-saving statement on slavery so as to hold the party to-
past	gether. They vaguely endorsed popular sovereignty and proposed that all questions in-

past	volving slavery in the territories be left up to the Supreme Court. When the convention adopted the Western platform, the delegations from eight lower South states withdrew from the hall. The remaining delegates
past	then proceeded to the selection of a candi-
past	date. Stephen A. Douglas led on every ballot, but he could not muster the two-thirds majority (of the original number of delegates) required by the party rules. Finally the manag-
past	ers adjourned the convention to meet again in Baltimore in June. At the Baltimore session,
past	most of the Southerners reappeared, only to walk out again. The rest of the Southerners
past perfect	had assembled at Richmond. The rump convention at Baltimore nominated Douglas. The
past	Southern bolters at Baltimore and the men in
past	Richmond nominated John C. Breckinridge of Kentucky.
past perfect	Sectionalism had at last divided the historic
past	Democratic party. There were now two Democratic candidates in the field, and although Douglas had supporters in the South and
past	Breckinridge in the North, one was the nominee of the Northern Democrats and the other of the Southern Democrats.

Current, Richard N., T. Harry Williams & Frank Freidel. Fifth Edition American History: A Survey, Volume I: To 1877, *Alfred A. Knopf, New York, 1979, pp. 370–371.*

The tense order runs between the past and the past perfect, with the present used for a definition. In the psychology selection below, also from Chapter 4, the tense order includes the past, the present, the conditional, and the future in an orderly and logical flow.

Past	We have talked about the common properties of a concept as if every property in a concept were true of every possible instance. Al-
Present	though some concepts, called *classical*, are like this, other concepts, called *probabalistic*,

Past
Conditional

Present

Past
Conditional
Present

Future

Present

Past

Present

are not. An example of a classical concept is a *bachelor*; every instance of this concept must have the properties of being adult, male, and unmarried. If someone described an adult as a *married bachelor*, you would probably think that person did not really understand the concept of bachelor. An example of a probabilistic concept is *bird*. Even though most people's concept of bird includes the properties of flying and chirping, not all birds fly (ostriches and penguins do not). So, if someone talked about a *nonflying bird*, you would find it perfectly acceptable. Most of our everyday concepts seem to be probabilistic (Smith and Medin, 1981).

For probabilistic concepts, some instances will have more of the concept's properties than other instances. Among birds, for example, a robin will have the property of flying, whereas an ostrich will not. And the more properties of a concept that an instance has, the more typical people consider that instance to be of the concept. Thus, people rate a robin as more typical of *bird* than an ostrich, they rate red apples as more typical than green ones of *apple* (since red seems to be a property of the concept *apple*), and so on. Not only do people judge one instance of a concept to be more typical than the other, they also classify the more typical one faster. The question "Is a robin a bird?" produces an immediate "yes"; "Is a chicken a bird?" takes longer. In addition to being classified faster, typical instances are more accessible in memory than less typical ones; when asked to list all the birds they can think of, people produce robin before ostrich (Rosch, 1978).

Atkinson, Atkinson, and Hilgard, op. cit. pp. 254–255.

These writers are not poor writers because they shift tenses; they are following a clear set of rules.

When we write, we have to deal with a complex relationship among events.

What had happened
What was happening
What happened
The result of what happened
What is happening
What happens
The generalization about happenings
What may happen
What might happen
What is going to happen
What will happen

In narratives and descriptions of a process, you need to make clear this relationship between events. As you bring in a new piece of information, you must work it into the order of events. As the list indicates, you will use most of the sequence automatically. But two kinds of events, the result of what happened and the generalization about what has happened, have conventional signals.

The result of what happened is often signalled by a *to* phrase (infinitive form) as in "the managers adjourned the convention *to meet again* ..." or "The Westerners hoped, however, to negotiate a face-saving statement on slavery, *so as to hold* the party together. The other signal is the *will have* or *would have* construction.

The generalization is nearly always signalled by the present tense, as the psychology passage shows. "An example of a probabilistic concept *is* bird." When you write a report of earlier research, you should separate who studied what when (using the past tense) from the findings (using the present tense).

How Tenses are Used in Academic Writing

We can make some generalizations on the basis of the following extracts from a research report. In looking at these extracts, you should concentrate on the tenses which the authors use to make their points. Some other stylistic features are peculiar to professional journals. You should not use them as guides for your writing.

1. When writers simply *report what was done*, they almost always use the *simple past tense*.

METHOD

Subjects

The Ss [subjects] *were* 40 undergraduate students in the University of Illinois who *participated* in partial fulfillment of the course requirements for introductory psychology.

Materials

Presentation and test lists *were constructed* from a pool of 140 sentences. Ninety-six of the sentences *were* the paired surface forms derived from 48 sentences written to allow an optional transformation. In the framework of transformational linguistics, one member of each of the pairs would be considered the un-transformed sentence, and the other the transform (i.e., derived by application of an optional transformation). Six different types of optional transformation *were included*, each represented by 8 different sentence pairs.

2. When writers *report on results* or *cite* obtained results as examples to support their generalizations, they typically use the *past tense*.

Citing supporting facts

The results show that sentences that admit an optional surface transformation are more difficult to recall correctly than control sentences with only one readily available surface sentence. All six classes of optional transforms sampled *showed* that this difficulty will occur in any class of sentences admitting optional surface transformations.

3. When writers *state something as an asserted fact* they typically use the *simple present tense*.

Assertion of fact	The results *show* that sentences that admit an optional surface transformation are more difficult to recall than control sentences with only one readily available surface sentence.

4. When writers *make a generalization* (something which is believed to hold for all cases and at all times), they typically use the *simple present tense*.

The results show that sentences that admit an optional transformation *are* more difficult to recall correctly than control. . . .

5. When writers *refer to a table, figure, chart, etc.,* they typically use the *simple present tense*.

Table 2 *gives* the percentages of responses in each scoring category.

But when they cite the figures in the tables, they typically use *simple past tense*. (see point 2)

6. When writers *describe established use of terms,* they typically use *simple present tense*.

Following Clark's notation, F_1 *refers* to the test statistic with Ss as a random effect.

7. When writers *refer to earlier research* which is assumed to be *relevant* to the present time or have *consequences* for present research, they typically use the *present perfect tense* combined with the

129

present instead of the simple past, which does not have such implications.

Sachs (1967) and Berg (1971) *have shown* with a recognition task that surface structures *are* difficult to detect, while semantic changes *are* easily identified.

Note how this sentence implies a much stronger generalization than would a corresponding sentence which used simple past *(showed ... were* more difficult to detect ... *were* easily identified). The former sentence shows that the writer is much more committed to believing that what is said is a general statement of how things actually are.

8. When writers *make a prediction* (formulate a hypothesis that will be tested), they typically use either the *simple future* and *should + verb*. The former implies a strong assertion and the latter implies something that ought to be a logical consequence of the theory.

If recall of sentences *involves* (Note: simple present tense in the premise) the reconstruction of syntactic relations and lexical items from an abstract semantic representation, then recall of sentences allowing optional transformation *should produce* particular difficulties.

If the text *is written* (simple present tense) in a style that the individual can produce, and there *is* only a single appropriate stylistic realization, then the text *will be recalled* correctly with few reconstructive errors.

Bock, Kathryn and Brewer, William F. "Reconstructive Recall in Sentences with Alternative Surface Structures," Journal of Experimental Psychology, *1974, Vol. 103, No. 5, pp. 837–843.* (Italics added)

From this analysis, you can see that there are some simple conventions about how academic papers use tenses.

In some cases, however, more than one possibility exists as in Point 7. In such cases, writers, perhaps sometimes not knowing it, convey subtle hints about the degree of their faith in what they are writing.

Although of course we do not expect you to memorize this chapter, you should refer to it and use some of its points as you revise your academic compositions. As we have said, you probably use many of these grammatical conventions unconsciously already. But you should also use your conscious knowledge to check your writing so that you can be sure you wrote what you intended.

We all have weaknesses and strong points in our knowledge of our own language resources. Thus, each of us needs to learn different things. Becoming aware of what we need to improve is important. Teachers can help you do this. Grammar books and books that give advice on good usage can serve as helpful reference books. But for effective learning, developing awareness and knowledge of language by ourselves is the best way. Thus we all have to generate a grammar style of our own, tailor-made for our needs, which we can consult easily. Our own grammar highlights such points that require conscious attention from us. You can construct your own grammar "rules" in your mind; better yet, you can write them down using the same method we used in describing how tenses are used in academic papers: "When I want to say . . ., I had better use . . . "

HOW TO MAKE A COMPOSITION OR ESSAY OR ESSAY EXAM DO WHAT YOU WANT IT TO DO—STYLISTIC METHODS TO INDIVIDUALIZE YOUR WRITING

7

Thus far in this book we have suggested how you may succeed in different kinds of academic writing. We have suggested types of structures that many students have found helpful in making their thoughts clear to teachers and other readers; we have also suggested some strategies to please readers. But we have not covered the ways you can use to make a composition your own; how you can imprint your personal stamp on what you write.

The specific assignment will determine some choices about writing. If your assignment is to classify information, you shouldn't write a story. A cause and effect paper requires different strategies than a comparison-contrast paper.

Suppose you were asked to write the answer to an exam question on the factors that led to Mexican independence from Spain. One choice you have is whether to concentrate on one factor and develop it — narrow the topic as you were taught in English classes — or to list as many factors as possible. Which course should you take? In an examination you should probably list as many items as possible even though the composition would not be focused. The reason is that in examinations your teacher expects you to give lots of information. In an essay, you can be more selective — rejecting minor factors and emphasizing major ones — but in most examinations you should tell everything you know and not be selective. This first choice arises from the situation and your sense of what you should do. There is, however, another kind of choice, one that suits your temperament or your sense of the temperament of your readers. Within this kind you have six *areas* of choice. We will illustrate these with responses to the writing assignments, *What should be done to improve my community?* We shall illustrate the differences with two outlines and five sets of paragraphs which exaggerate each area of choice.

Choice 1

Should I include many aspects of the topic in my writing, or should I select one and develop it?

Inclusive Outline Covers Many Aspects
    A. 1. My community has a shortage of housing.
         a. Many families are crowded in buildings that are too small.
         b. The community should build more houses.
      2. The streets and buildings are in poor repair.
         a. Every street has holes full of water.
         b. The public buildings need paint.
         c. The community should make repairs.
      3. The schools are located away from where people live.

       a. As the community has grown the schools have not moved close to the new housing.
       b. The community should either build new neighborhood schools or improve public transportation.
  4. Little opportunity exists for young people.
       a. Because there are few jobs outside of one factory and some shops, young people must move away.
       b. The community should attract new businesses.

Selective Outline Develops One Aspect

B. 1. As my community has grown in size, it has not provided enough opportunity for work.
       a. There is only one factory which has jobs, and these jobs are dull.
       b. Young people can only work for their families if they want to stay.
       c. As a result, young people leave the community.
  2. The community should provide more opportunities.
       a. It could atttract new factories and shops.
       b. It could create an employment center.
       c. It could provide training for young people to get ahead.

The second outline expands on the fourth point of the first outline, giving details of the problems and offering some specific suggestions. Because the problem of employment is seen as only one of a number of problems in the first outline, the writer would summarize that material. As we suggested at the beginning of this chapter, the first outline is probably better for an examination, which usually asks you to give a great deal of information, but does not expect you to elaborate on it. In an out-of-class essay or a term paper, however, focusing on one aspect is usually better because you can develop your topic in some depth. You might well take the other points — lack of housing, poor location of schools, and lack of repair and subordinate them to the point about opportunity to work. Could you show that these other three problems contribute to the lack of employment? Might they be the reasons that industries do not want to relocate in the community? If you can bring the other aspects of the topic to bear upon the major one you have chosen, your paper will be more focused. If you cannot relate them to that topic, leave them out or say that you are not going to discuss them. In most academic writing except for examinations, you will be more successful if you select one aspect as the thesis of your paper and develop that aspect thoroughly.

Choice 2

Should I write abstractly or concretely?

ABSTRACT: KEEPING THE TOPIC GENERAL

Group characteristics

The most serious problem my community faces is that people do not care for appearance of the community. It seems that both the *individual citizens* and the *local government* consider other things more important than making the community an attractive place to live. Older *buildings* deteriorate, and when *new buildings* go up the signs of construction may remain for *long periods* after the work is finished. This *lack of care* is visible in the streets and the various public places around the community. The problem does not appear to be a *lack of money* but a lack of interest.

CONCRETE: MAKING THE TITLE SPECIFIC

Individual details

The most serious problem in my community is the ugliness which makes the community an unattractive place to live. *A person* walking down any street can see houses with *broken windows* or with *junk* piles around them. In the main part of town, the *two public build-ings* are dirty and the paint is peeling from the walls. The *new town garage* finished *a year ago* and now in use, has *piles of leftover con-struction lumber* lying in the yard, and the dirt *around the building* is still piled in the mound the bulldozer made. Every street needs to have *potholes* filled, most benches in *the town park* need repairs, and the plumbing in the public lavatory has not worked for a year. The community seems rich enough; *it buys new trucks.* The government and the taxpayers do not seem to care, and so nobody else does either.

When you write an essay, making the choice between these two approaches is not easy. Note that in each case the writer has supported the thesis with examples, as any good writer does, but the first deals with types, and the second names names — is more specific and detailed. In part your ap-proach will depend on what your teacher wants. Some will want you to name specifically named objects or give very detailed descriptions of events. Some others prefer you to write about types of objects or events, particularly if they are interested in the logic of your argument and its universality. Each approach has its own special problems. If you spend a lot of space and time on details, giving the minutest picture of what things look like or sound like or smell like, or all the events in a battle, or all the numbers in a statistical report, the reader may tend to forget the point you are making, because you have forgotten to remind the reader or perhaps you have forgotten yourself. On the other hand, a total lack of detail may make your writing appear bland and the reader will want some example so as to see whether your generalization applies in a specific case.

So you have to juggle your writing between the two extremes. Remember the saying about some people, "He can't see the forest for the trees." The counter saying holds true as well, "She can't see the trees for the forest." Again, in your writing make sure that your general point is clear. Don't lose it, particularly not in an examination. But be sure that you give enough details to show that you have read the assigned material and have the specific facts in hand. If you make the general point that there are five causes of an economic slump, be sure to specify what the five are.

> Paragraph I: Thesis Statement (5 causes) enumerated in the paragraph
> Paragraph II: Cause 1
> Paragraph III: Cause 2
> Paragraph IV: Cause 3
> Paragraph V: Cause 4
> Paragraph VI: Cause 5
> Paragraph VII: Summary and discussion of causes

Choice 3

Should the writing be figurative and suggestive or literal and down-to-earth?

FIGURATIVE: USES METAPHOR AND SIMILE

Simile to set up the mood
Specific simile

The young people in my town feel *like animals in a circus or in a pet store.* Some of us girls who are still at home are *like caged birds*, fed, made pretty, and taught to be objects of admiration. We cannot escape and try our wings by going off on trips or going away to another college. We sometimes feel that our parents keep us in cages until some man finds us to set us free by marrying us and then putting us in another cage. Some of my friends have broken their wings trying to escape and become dull and listless. The boys,

Second simile

on the other hand, are *like lion cubs* being trained to respond to the commands of a

Two similes brought together

ringmaster. The factory whistle is the ringmaster's whip, completely commanding their lives. They look at their parents, the old mangy animals who are now completely subdued and simply go through the motions, and wonder how long it will be before they are like them. *For the young animals and the birds* it will be even worse than for the older ones. We have had a taste of freedom because of school and many other conveniences. We can see the cages and the ringmaster. But can we escape?

LITERAL: USES ORDINARY LANGUAGE

Literal description

My friend Misa feels as I do that our community offers no opportunity for us and our friends. We often talk to each other and discuss the arguments and reasons we will present to our families for leaving here. There are no jobs for us here. No future is possible here except to join the crowds of other people, young and old who are hungry and listless. *The old factory whistle sounds at the same* time every day, signaling old, tired, bored workers to produce the exported goods. The work days are long, the money is little, but the boredom is great for those fortunate enough to have a job. The officials accept the situation here as inevitable and fixed. Life goes on as it always has with no changes except declines in the quality of life. *Opportunities are lacking for young people* in all areas, personal, social, economic and political. The youth are doomed here to a life worse than their mothers and fathers had. The community has no plans and goals for the future, no leaders to guide. The problems are great.

Compare to whistle above

Compare to old animals above

Clearly the choice between these two approaches is determined by the course and the teacher. In only a few courses of which we are aware does a teacher actively encourage a figurative style. Usually those courses are in literature or writing. For most of the sciences and social sciences, however, teachers appear to prefer a literal approach to the topic and a minimum of metaphor. However, don't be afraid to use a metaphor that will make your point clearer and more vivid to your reader. In Chapter 4 we quoted a section from an historical essay in which the writer uses the following metaphor:

When the soldiers marched off to the 1914 war, so did the words. The surviving soldiers came back, four years later, harrowed and beaten. *In a real sense, the words did not. They remained at the front and built between the German mind and the facts a wall of myth. They launched* the first of those big lies on which so much of modern Germany has been nurtured: the lie of "the stab in the back." The heroic German armies had not been defeated; they had been stabbed in the back by "traitors, degenerates, and Bolsheviks." The Treaty of Versailles was not an awkward attempt by a ravaged Europe to pick up some of the pieces but a scheme of cruel vengeance imposed on Germany by its greedy foes. The responsibility for unleashing war lay with Russia or Austria or the colonial machinations of "perfidious England," not with Prussian Germany.

Steiner, op. cit., p. 98. (Italics added)

The words, of course, are not alive, but the metaphor of the words remaining "at the front," building "a wall," and launching "big lies," gives the reader a sense of the dramatic power of language. The metaphor helps the reader to better visualize a process.

If you use such metaphors, save them for the points at which you think what you are explaining may be unclear to your reader. What metaphors have helped you understand what you read? They may help your reader too. A metaphor can help your reader build a bridge from the known (soldiers) to the unknown (words), like the bridge we built in this sentence to explain how a writer can help a reader. Even so-called "dead" metaphors like *bridge* help readers understand.

Choice 4

Should I be personal or impersonal?

PERSONAL: I REFER TO MYSELF

Personal detail

In order to describe the main problem of my community, *I* shall tell you about my family. *I live at home with my mother and father and an older brother.* I have two older sisters but they have left home and gone to the city, one to work as a secretary, the other to work in a bank. My older brother is about to leave also.

Sense of dialogue with reader

You see, my father is foreman in the factory and my mother works at home taking care of the family and the small garden. The factory is the only place where there are jobs unless you want to be a farmer or you happen to own one of the shops. My uncle owns a shop and his children work for him so that there are not jobs for others. The factory is not very big and the work is dull. If a person wants to improve, the way my sisters and brother do, a person has to leave. I feel this is a nice town,

Personal feeling

and I have many friends here, but *I also want* to do something different. I suspect I will move away when I finish school.

IMPERSONAL: I KEEP MYSELF OUT OF IT

Focus on community not the writer

The major problem of the community is, I think, a lack of opportunity for young people. The community has three shops: a grocery, a small clothing shop, and a small hardware and tool shop, as well as a branch of the bank. There is also a small factory that employs about seventy-five people. Apart

Groups of people but not the writer

from that the only other work that people do in the community is farming and teaching in the school. There are *more young people* than there are jobs, and many of the jobs are boring, particularly if people want to get ahead in the world. *Several of the young people,* I believe, are content to work in the factory or for their parents in a shop or on the farms. *Only a few,* however, want to teach in the school. As a result of this situation, about *half of the young people* who finish school leave the community.

In many ways, this choice is the most difficult to make, and depends most on your audience. In some courses you will take, the teacher will insist that you keep your opinions to yourself; other teachers will encourage you to share your feelings and impressions. Nevertheless, even when you use the impersonal form (third person), you make your knowledge, thoughts, and opinions known to your reader. You cannot help yourself; you make the choice of what to say and which words you use. When you are asked to write a paper, you state what you think about the topic.

We can give some advice on how best to handle your presentations of yourself.

1. Give only the relevant information about yourself. Don't spend a lot of time on your life history.
2. Distinguish among the following expressions; each says something about your commitment to a point and how you can support it.

    I think — gives your ideas or interpretations which you can support with reasons. You announce that you are going to use logic.

    I believe or In my opinion — gives your beliefs and opinions which you can support with other opinions. You announce that you may cite an authority or give a reason that is not entirely logical.

I feel — gives your emotional reactions which are hard to support. You announce that you are writing as an individual, are willing to listen to others, and even perhaps to accept their arguments.

3. Use personal experience to support or contradict a generalization, but remember that your reader may see your experience as an exception. Your experience is not enough on which to base a generalization about all people; you should try to find confirmation outside of your own experience.

Choice 5

Should I write logically or digressively, adding an informal note that shows how I think?

LOGICAL: FOLLOWS THE TOPIC FORMALLY

One of the first things the leaders in my community could do to make the community more attractive is to create a campaign to

If-then logic   make the houses more attractive. *If* the leaders were to award prizes for the family that did the best job of fixing its house and cleaning the surrounding grounds, most families would accept the challenge. After *first* giving awards to families, the community could *then* expand the plan to public buildings and parks. Prizes and awards could go to groups of volunteers who would undertake the work of fixing these places and making them pretty.

Counter-argument *One might argue* that these volunteers would
refuted   not want to pay money for materials, *but to* solve the problem the community leaders could supply materials such as tools and

Logical conclusion paint. The cost to an individual or a group
to refutation would, *therefore*, only be the cost of time. *If*
If-then logic *everyone* were to join, moreover, the amount
of time would not be too great for any one
Summary of if-then person. *By following a process* of individual
process awards to group awards, the leaders could
help make my community attractive.

DIGRESSIVE: ADD INFORMAL DETAILS
The leaders of the community could make the
place more attractive by helping people fix up
and clean up their own houses and community buildings. I mean that people probably
just need a start. Imagine what would happen
if the leaders gave prizes to the people who
help the most. One prize might go to the
neatest garden area. Then another prize
Digressive might go to the prettiest house. *It would not*
explanation *be for the original design, but for the best*
cleaning, fixing, and painting. Then, other
people could win an award for picking up the
rubbish in the town square. It is usually filthy,
After-thought that with trash in the bushes. *The town leaders*
leads to next *could give out paint and tools to help, by the*
section *way.* They could lend them to people to work
on their own homes on days when the town
workers do not need them. At the end, it
would be nice to see banners and flags above
the streets. The whole community would be
bright and shiny. You would agree it would be
a pleasant place to live, and the leaders and
the people would have a common goal and a
sense of pride.

Like the preceding choice this one depends on
whether you think your reader wants to see how you as an
individual think with all your quirks and turns or wants to
see whether you can create a formal logical argument or
description. The second example resembles an informal
conversation and could be diagrammed as in Figure 7-1.

Figure 7-1   **Informal conversation**

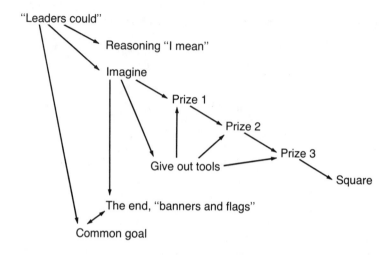

It all fits like a mosaic and urges the reader to imagine a picture. Compare Figure 7-2 to the one for the first example which is less complex and uses logical terms.

Figure 7-2   **Concise, logical approach**

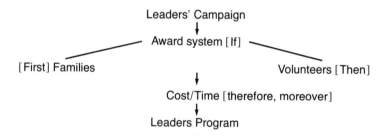

In some cases you may find it necessary to give your reader information that you cannot place easily. You know your reader needs the information, but it does not fit in your paragraph. One solution is to put the information in parenthesis; another is to use an explanatory footnote. In the following section of an essay, the author, Stephen Jay Gould, explains how one divides living organisms into species. Gould uses three parenthetical statements as digressions for three specific purposes and one general purpose (to be informal):

We maintain similar practices in our own folk taxonomy. Edible mollusks are "shellfish," but Linnaean species all have common names. I well remember the reprimand I received from a New England shipmate when I applied the informal scientific term 1 "clam" to all bivalved mollusks (to him a clam is only the steamer, *Mya arenaria*): "A quahog is a quahog, a clam is a clam, and a scallop is a scallop."
The evidence of folk taxonomy is persuasive for the modern world. Unless the tendency to divide organisms into Linnaean 2 species reflects a neurological style wired into all of us (an interesting proposition, but one that I doubt), the world of nature is, in some fundamental sense, really divided into reasonably dis- 3 crete packages of creatures as a result of evolution. (I do not, of course, deny that our propensity for classifying in the first place reflects something about our brains, their inherited capacities, and the limited ways in which complexity may be ordered and made sensible. I merely doubt that such a definite procedure as classification into Linnaean species could reflect the constraints of our mind alone, and not of nature.)

Stephen Jay Gould, The Panda's Thumb, W.W. Norton & Co., Inc., New York, 1980, p. 212.

The first digression, about the steamer clam, enables the writer to show that the shipmate thinks as an eater and not as a scientist. The second digression serves to show that the *unless* proposition is ridiculous, and the third goes back to the second to discuss whether classes exist in the brain or in the world and suggests it is both. The material outside the parenthesis argues that people have always seen classes and made taxonomies, while the material inside is a series of digressions on whether these taxonomies are created by people or are in nature. If the writer had not used parentheses, the paragraphs would have confused the reader. He could have used a footnote for the first and the third, but using one would have taken the reader away from the main text too long. Footnotes are useful if you think the information is not really important. Keep the information in the text if you want your reader to have it there, but signal that it is secondary with parentheses or an expression such as *by the way* or *incidentally.*

Choice 6

Should I write seriously or humorously?

SERIOUS TONE

Matter-of-fact language

There are a number of problems in my community but most of them would take a lot of time and money to solve. There is, however, one problem which *is an acute one which citizens could resolve without spending large* sums of money. That *is the problem of boredom. Nothing exciting ever seems* to happen in the community. Yet, this need not be so. Some *creative ideas* and *community spirit* could change a lot. The mayor could set up a committee of both older and younger people to recommend new activities. *These might* include choirs for children and for adults and perhaps an amateur orchestra or band and an amateur theater group. Athletically oriented citizens might set up challenge matches or games between blocks or districts. People might revive old handicraft skills and stage shows demonstrating how people produced goods in the past and what these products looked like. People might help to lay out a jogging track in a park or a forest. These few examples suggest what citizens might do to change boredom to pleasurable activity. Local groups would devise different solutions to suit their special circumstances.

HUMOROUS TONE

Exaggerated language

Any problems in our community? Are your kidding? *There are nothing but problems.* We *have so many problems* that we could easily organize a sale, sell a lot at a bargain, and still have more than enough for home consumption.The greatest problem is boredom. Griping about this problem never did any good, however. What we need is a lot of action backed with a pinch of thinking. We have to be careful with thinking, though. It might develop like a habit, and nothing good ever came from too much thinking. But one solution for boredom comes to mind. We know bores make the town boring. The mayor might set up a *committee consisting of the greatest bores* in town. They would never be able to finish their work, and we would never hear from them again. That alone would go a long way to improve local conversation. Those with no ear for music but with a great desire for performing in public might be asked to form a choir or a band to be led by a very exacting musician. They *would spend all their time practicing and torturing each other but not the rest of us.* Other bores might be encouraged to take up football or skiing. Soon most of them would *be lying in a hospital* with a broken leg. Several weeks of relief! These are only a few examples of what might be done to combat boredom. Different kinds of solutions would have to be devised to cope with a local variety of bores.

Like the figurative and personal choices, the choice as to whether you should be humorous is a matter of temperament and involves some risks in academic writing. Gould's digressions were humorous, but he made his humor serve a point; so did some of the writers we quoted in Chapters 4 and 5. Humor, as you probably know, is tricky. No two people laugh at the same joke. Your audience may take your humor the wrong way, particularly if you use humor to make fun of another person or groups of people. At the same time, a teacher who has been reading thirty compositions on the same topic may appreciate a bit of humor, and the writer's grade may go up. Humor can often make a dull topic more fun to write and more fun to read. In much academic writing a small touch of humor will make the medicine of the message go down a little easier. Just don't try to be the life of the class. Save that role for the teacher.

How do you make these choices? Two criteria you should use are: Which style fits me and the way I look at the world? Which style do I think will win the approval of my reader? We cannot answer the first question, but we can give some tentative answers to the second. In general, teachers, unlike most people reading what you write, will question your intention and meaning. Usually, also, teachers have to read a good number of papers and often get bored. You can impress your teacher if your paper adds new information or presents a novel slant. If the assignment calls for your own views, a personal, figurative, or a humorous approach may appeal to your reader—but never use a "cute" approach. With some topics, particularly on examinations where your instructor wants information, an inclusive, specific approach works best. In most academic subjects a tightly logical style will succeed better than a digressive one. In philosophy, economics, and political science when theoretical papers are assigned an abstract approach will probably please a reader more than a concrete one.

But none of our suggestions are absolute prescriptions. You should make your choice based on your sense of: 1) How you like to write, 2) What you think the assignment calls for, and 3) What you think will impress your reader favorably. In the exercise section, we give you a method of diagnosing assignments that will help you plan your writing. In many courses you will have more than one opportunity to write for your teacher, but in a good number you will have only one composition assignment. If you cannot ask a former student what the teacher is like, we suggest you take the middle path.

Some Concluding Suggestions

Some general points apply to all human communication including writing. We humans have to cooperate in order to communicate, and we have problems in spite of our best efforts to be cooperative. We can never say or write everything we want to communicate in a message. Our listener or reader must make guesses and inferences about the missing parts. In most situations our listener or reader guesses and infers automatically and quite successfully because we are members of the same speech community; we share the same culture.

To cooperate, you as a writer have to recognize and admit that you have certain obligations to the reader and vice versa. When the purpose is to convey information, you have a responsibility to write so that the text is informative, truthful, relevant, and clear. You have to write enough for your audience to get the meaning. Too little information may cause misunderstanding and too many facts may be boring. Writing for your teachers is especially difficult. They usually have read the material you have; they will often be bored if you tell them all the obvious points. In particular, a summary of a book or article that you have both read should be short and give only the main points relevant to your paper. As a writer you also have an obligation to convey a truthful message. Truth, however, is not enough. If you make truthful statements and do not relate them to the task at hand, you distract your reader with irrelevant matters. Finally, since your goal is to inform your readers, you should try to make your text as clear as possible.

As this book suggests, many ways are open to you to fulfill these general requirements. The choice of ways depends upon the situation. What is sufficiently informative in normal everyday communication may not be specific enough in an examination where the examiner expects you to demonstrate as much of your knowledge as you can. In every academic writing situation you have to make clear to yourself what the requirements are. You may help yourself if you make a set of guidelines to help you remember to do certain things while planning what to write, while evaluating what you have written, and while making revisions.

No rules or guidelines are equally appropriate for everybody. All writers have individual preferences, and they all have different kinds of experiences, different kinds of knowledge, and different strong and weak points. Some writers like to plan everything carefully while some prefer to write spontaneously and do a lot of careful reading and revision of their texts. But all writers have to develop their own guidelines that are comfortable for them. In most cases, readers don't care *how* writers write compositions; readers are mainly interested in the quality of the finished composition itself.

Since you have to make your own guidelines, to help you we have listed examples of some decisions writers have to make. Select those you think you need to follow.

What I Need to Do Before I Starting Writing on This Assignment

I had better just be calm and try my best.
In this course the teacher expects me to pay special attention to these points while writing: . . . .

My main point will be this . . . . I had better avoid trying to be humorous. This teacher prefers us to . . . and this teacher does not like us to . . . .

I had better write as neatly and clearly as I can. I had better type my paper since my handwriting is not so legible.

I had better make an outline first.

I had better concentrate on discussing only a few central topics.

I will first deal with A, then with B and finally with C.

In the concluding section I will repeat my main thesis in a slightly different form.

I had better write . . . paragraphs (pages).

When I am finished with the final draft I had better read through the text twice; once for checking the content (ideas) and once for checking the form and language. I had better be very critical.

I had better check punctuation and spelling.

I had better hand in my paper on time.

What I Need to Keep in Mind While Checking My Text as I Write or Between Drafts

Readers (my reader) may not realize from what I have written that this is an important point.

Readers (my reader) will probably not be interested in this.

I think that this point will interest readers/my reader.

Readers (my reader) may not believe this.

Readers (my reader) may not understand what I am trying to say here.

This will not convince my readers (my reader).

This is a good point.

This is a good sentence.

This does not sound right/good.

I could say this much better.

I am introducing irrelevant points here.

This detail does not support my point.

This sentence is not well connected with the previous one.

This idea does not fit here. Its place is in the second (third . . .) paragraph, before/after the place where I talk about . . . .

These facts do not lead anywhere. I must put in a generalization.

This conclusion cannot logically be drawn from what I have written. I had forgotten to say that . . . .

I need to remind my reader of my thesis here.

This word is not appropriate in this kind of a paper.

This is too impersonal. I better say what I think.

This is too personal/subjective. I had better stick to the "facts" and to what others (the "experts") have said about this.

This is too wordy.

I need to expand this point.

Even I cannot read what it says here. I had better erase this and write it more neatly.

What I Need to Do To My Text

I will not change this. I will leave this as it is.

I had better give an example.

I had better leave this out. It does not tell anything new.

I had better cross out this sentence and rewrite it entirely.

I had better add here the idea that . . . .

I had better change wording here.

I had better start a new paragraph here.

I had better write more. This is much too short.
I had better give reasons for my opinion here.

A Final Checklist

Did I put my name on the paper?
Did I leave enough of a margin?
Did I spell the instructor's name right?
Did I get someone to check the paper for typos?
Is everything legible?
Are all the references there?
Are the pages numbered?
Is it stapled or paper-clipped?
Did I keep a copy for myself?
Ok? Now I can hand it in.

HOW TO FIND OUT IF YOU'VE LEARNED HOW TO READ AND WRITE BETTER

The following exercises deal with matters related to certain parts of this book where we think that you might well do some limbering up before you actually tackle a writing assignment. In some cases we give a model for you to follow and no answer, because we think that you can figure out the answer given the material you will really have to work with. In some other cases we have created some exercises that have answers, and they are printed next to the exercise. Of course you can look at the answer as you are doing the exercise. But the important point is that you should think not simply of the answer but of the reason why that answer is best. There we won't help you. You can write your reasons to us. We would be glad to hear from you. If you write use:

College Editorial Department
Harcourt Brace Jovanovich Publishers
1250 Sixth Ave.
San Diego, California 92101

Exercise 1 — (See Chapters 1 and 2)
Diagnosing a Writing Assignment

Many of the writing assignments you will receive in college will give little more than a topic and perhaps certain other information. Before you begin to work on the assignment, you can figure out more information about it by asking yourself some questions. You might also ask the instructor to give some additional information if you cannot work it out for yourself. Below are the major areas of information about an assignment that will shape what you write.

1. The Domain Cell: Look at Table 1-1 again, which we reprint here as Table 1-1A, with the cells blank to help you answer the questions in the first group. Can you put the assignment in one of these cells? What kind of cognitive processing does it require? What is Primary Content? Answering those two questions will help you locate the column. What appears to be the dominant purpose? Who is the primary audience? The answers to those two questions should locate the row. Now you have a good idea of the kind of work you will have to do.

2. The Content Area: What is the subject area for which you are writing? What particular aspect of the subject area is indicated in the assignment?

3. Content Cues: Does the assignment suggest anything about how much information you are going to

Table 1-1A

GENERAL MODEL OF WRITTEN DISCOURSE

Dominant Intention/Purpose	Cognitive Processing — Primary Content / Primary Audience	Reproduce		Organize/Reorganize		Invent/Generate
		Facts	Ideas	Events	Visual images, facts, mental states, ideas	Ideas, mental states, alternative worlds
To learn (metalingual)	Self					
To convey emotions, feelings (emotive)	Self, Others					
To inform (referential)	Others					
To convince/persuade (conative)	Others					
To entertain, delight, please (poetic)	Others					
To keep in						

have to provide? Where can you get the information? Is there a special angle on the topic that is implied by the assignment?

4. Audience: Is the audience specified? Is it the instructor? another member of the class? someone else? How much does the audience know? What are the audience's attitudes towards the topic?

5. Structural and Procedural Cues: Does the assignment say anything about the organization of the writing?

6. Format: Is there any specification as to length, footnote style, margins, or the like?

7. Criteria: How will the writing be judged? Are there any specific criteria in the assignment?

We have worked out the answers for a sample assignment on the next page.

GEOGRAPHY 106 — Write a paper of five to six pages in which you explain the effects of industrialization on the climate of cities. In your paper you should discuss both temperature and precipitation effects and the most likely causes of these effects.

DOMAIN CELL: Invent/generate ideas in order to inform or to convince an instructor. This means you must not only reorganize the material you know about climate and industrialization, you must also argue that one or more sets of causes is more probable than another.

CONTENT AREA: Geography, climatology. The assignment suggests two specific aspects of the topic: temperature and precipitation. Are there other aspects?

CONTENT CUES: Is the information needed to answer the question in the textbook and lecture notes? Were there references in the textbook that might help me? The question seems to suggest multiple causes and effects. Should I look elsewhere to see if there might be other causes?

Perhaps there is something in the general chapter on climate.

AUDIENCE: The assignment doesn't specify one, but who usually reads the papers? Does the instructor seem to be an authority on this topic? Does the instructor favor certain ideas? Review my lecture notes.

STRUCTURAL AND PROCEDURAL CUES: The topic calls for cause and effect: What is the best organization of a cause and effect paper? Should I save the cause I favor for the conclusion?

FORMAT: Five to six pages. Does the text suggest footnote form?

CRITERIA: It looks as if the paper suggests that reasoning about causes is important. I should check my reasoning.

There may be other matters that you would want to raise. But having analyzed this assignment, we think that you could write with greater confidence.

Now try out an analysis on an assignment you have received.

Exercise 2 (Chapters 2 and 3):
Determining the Organizational Pattern of a Text

1. Look at pages 2–4 of this volume.
2. Select the words or phrases that indicate the organizational pattern of the section.
3. Check Table 2-2 on page 19. What pattern dominates the section? Cause-effect? Thesis support? Classification? Process? Comparison–contrast?

Exercise 3 (Chapter 3):
Determining the Purpose of a Textbook

In Chapter 5, we presented the introduction of a philosophy text by Morris Weitz. In that introduction, Weitz showed how he turned a topic into questions and a thesis. Look at the introduction to one of your textbooks or required readings, and answer the following questions:

1. What is the topic?
2. What questions about the topic does the writer raise?
3. What assumptions appear to underlie these questions?
4. What thesis is the book setting forth?

Exercise 4 (Chapter 3):
Outlining and Summarizing

1. Reread Chapter 2 of this book. Write an outline of the chapter.
2. Write a summary of the chapter in no more than 150 words.
3. Can you reduce the summary to 50 words and still retain the essential part of the message? Note what kind of changes you made in condensing the text, for instance, in:
   sentence patterns (e.g. collapsing sentences)
   vocabulary (e.g. superordinate or general terms)
   pronouns (reference)
   Could you improve your 50-word summary by making some further revisions in sentence patterns, vocabulary, or reference?

Exercise 5 (Chapters 4 and 5):
Classification and Organization of Material

Look at these three sections from Roget's *Thesaurus* and determine what types of organization they use. Keep in mind that when Peter Mark Roget wrote his *Thesaurus of Words and Phrases* in the early nineteenth century, he decided to classify all of the English language by content. Then he could put the words in groups expressing similar ideas. Figures E1, E2, and E3 from *(The Original Roget's Thesaurus of English Words and Phrases, Revised by Robert A. Deutch, O.B.E., St. Martin's Press, New York, 1965.)* are his general "Plan of Classification," one of his "Tabular Synopsis of Categories," and one of the entries. Where did he have to modify his system? Do the words in the entry all fall under the category? Could you use them interchangeably?

If you do not have a *Thesaurus*, you should get one that is arranged this way. The classifications will help your writing just as much as the synonyms.

Exercise 6 (Chapters 4 and 5):
Determining a Structure

Read each selection and determine which of the six basic structures it seems to fit best. Which structure have we left out?

Nay, self-education in any shape, in the most restricted sense, is preferable to a system of teaching which, professing so much, really does so little for the mind. Shut your College gates against the votary of knowledge, throw him back upon the searchings and the efforts of his own mind; he will gain by being spared an entrance into your Babel. Few, indeed, there are who can dispense with the stimulus and support of instructors, or will do any thing at all, if left to themselves. And fewer still (though such great minds are to be found), who will not, from such unassisted attempts, contract a self-reliance and a self-esteem, which are not only moral evils, but serious hindrances to the attainment of truth. And next to none, perhaps, or none, who will not be reminded from time to time of the disadvantage under which they lie, by their imperfect grounding, by the breaks, deficiencies, and irregularities of their knowledge, by the eccentricity of opinion and

Figure E1   Part of Roget's Plan of Classification

PLAN OF CLASSIFICATION

*The numbers in the right-hand column relate
to the present edition*

Class and Division	Section	Nos.
I ABSTRACT	**I Existence**	1–8
RELATIONS	**II Relation**	9–25
	III Quantity	26–59
	IV Order	60–84
	V Number	85–107
	VI Time	108–142
	VII Change	143–155
	VIII Causation	156–182
II SPACE	**I Space in General**	183–194
	II Dimensions	195–242
	III Form	243–264
	IV Motion	265–318
III MATTER	**I Matter in General**	319–323
	II Inorganic Matter	324–357
	III Organic Matter	358–446
IV INTELLECT	**I General**	447–452
Division (I)	**II Precursory Conditions and**	453–465
FORMATION OF	**Operations**	
IDEAS	**III Materials for Reasoning**	466–474
	IV Reasoning Processes	475–479
	V Results of Reasoning	480–504
	VI Extension of Thought	505–511
	VII Creative Thought	512–513
Division (II)	**I Nature of Ideas**	
COMMUNICATION	**Communicated**	514–521

[xlv]

Figure E-2 A Partial Tabular Synopsis of Categories from Roget

TABULAR SYNOPSIS OF CATEGORIES

CLASS IV. INTELLECT

DIVISION (I). FORMATION OF IDEAS

Section	*Head*	
I Intellectual Operations in General		
	447 Intellect	(450)
	448 Non-intellect	(450a)
	449 Thought	(451)
	450 Absence of thought	(452)
	451 Idea	(453)
	452 Topic	(454)
II Precursory Conditions and Operations		
	453 Curiosity	(455)
	454 Incuriosity	(456)
	455 Attention	(457)
	456 Inattention	(458)
	457 Carefulness	(459)
	458 Negligence	(460)
	459 Inquiry	(461)
	460 Answer	(462)
	461 Experiment	(463)
	462 Comparison	(464)
	463 Discrimination	(465)
	464 Indiscrimination	(465a)
	465 Measurement	(466)
III Materials for Reasoning		
	466 Evidence	(467)
	467 Counter-evidence	(468)
	468 Qualification	(469)
degrees of evidence	469 Possibility	(470)
	470 Impossibility	(471)
	471 Probability	(472)

[lx]

Figure E-3   An Entry from Roget

446–448

tinct.

Vb. *disappear,* vanish, do the vanishing trick; dematerialize, melt into thin air; evanesce, evaporate 338vb. *vaporize;* dissolve, melt, melt away 337vb. *liquefy;* waste, consume, wear away, wear off, dwindle, dwindle to vanishing point 37vb. *decrease;* fade, fade out, pale 426vb. *lose color;* fade away 114vb. *be transient;* be occulted, suffer *or* undergo an eclipse 419vb. *be dim;* disperse, dissipate, diffuse, scatter 75vb. *be dispersed;* absent oneself, fail to appear, play truant 190vb. *be absent;* go, be gone, depart 296vb. *decamp;* run away, get a. 667vb. *escape;* hide, lie low, be in hiding 523vb. *lurk;* cover one's tracks, leave no trace 525vb. *conceal;* be lost to sight 444vb. *be unseen;* retire from view, seclude oneself 883vb. *seclude;* become extinct, leave not a rack behind 2vb. *pass away;* make disappear, erase, dispel 550vb. *obliterate.*

See: 2, 37, 51, 75, 114, 190, 296, 337, 338, 418, 419, 426, 444, 523, 525, 542, 550, 667 883.

447 Intellect

N. *intellect,* mind, psyche, psychic organism, mentality; understanding, intellection, conception; thinking principle, intellectual faculty, cogitative f.; rationality, reasoning power; reason, discursive r., association of ideas 475n. *reasoning;* philosophy 449n. *thought;* awareness, sense, consciousness, self-c., stream of c. 455n. *attention;* cognizance, noesis, perception, apperception, percipience, insight; extrasensory perception, instinct 476n. *intuition;* flair, judgment 463n. *discrimination;* noology, intellectualism, intellectuality; mental capacity, brains, parts, wits, senses, sense, gray matter 498n. *intelligence;* great intellect, genius; mental evolution, psychogenesis; seat of thought, organ of t., brain, anterior t., cerebrum; hinder brain, little b., cerebellum; medulla oblongata; meninx, pia mater, dura m., arachnoid 213n. *head;* sensorium, sensory 818n. *feeling.*

psychology, science of mind, psychics, metapsychology, metapsychics; parapsychology, abnormal psychology 503n. *psychopathy;* psychosomatics, Freudianism, Freudian psychology, Jungian p., Adlerian p.; Gestalt psychology, Gestalt theory, configurationism, behaviorism; empirical psychology; psychography, psychometry, psychoanalysis; psychopathology, psychiatry, psychotherapy 658n. *therapy;* psychophysiology, psychophysics, psychobiology.

psychologist, psychoanalyst, psychiatrist, psychotherapist, psychopathologist, mental specialist, alienist, mad doctor 658n. *doctor.*

spirit, soul, mind, inner m., inner sense, second s.; heart, heart's core, breast, bosom, inner man 224n. *interiority;* double, ka, ba, genius 80n. *self;* psyche, pneuma, id, ego, superego, self, subliminal s., the unconscious, the subconscious; personality, dual p., multiple p., split p. 503n. *psychopathy;* spiritualism, spiritism, psychomancy, psychic research 984n. *occultism;* spiritualist, occultist.

Adj. *mental,* thinking, endowed with reason, reasoning 475adj. *rational;* cerebral, intellectual, conceptive, noological; noetic, conceptual, abstract; theoretical 512adj. *suppositional;* unconcrete 320adj. *immaterial;* perceptual, percipient, perceptive; cognitive, cognizant 490adj. *knowing;* conscious, self-c., subjective.

psychic, psychical, psychological; subconscious, subliminal; spiritualistic, mediumistic, psychomantic 984adj. *psychic;* spiritual, otherworldly 320adj. *immaterial.*

Vb. *cognize,* perceive, apperceive 490vb. *know;* realize, sense, become aware of, become conscious of; objectify 223vb. *externalize;* note 438vb. *see;* advert, mark 455vb. *notice;* ratiocinate 475vb. *reason;* understand 498vb. *be wise;* conceptualize, intellectualize 449vb. *think;* conceive, invent 484vb. *discover;* ideate 513vb. *imagine;* appreciate 480vb. *estimate.*

See: 80, 213, 223, 224, 320, 438, 449, 455, 463, 475, 480, 490, 498, 503, 512, 513, 658, 818, 948, 984.

448 Non-intellect

N. *non-intellect,* unintellectuality; brute creation 365n. *animality;* vegetation 366n. *vegetability;* inanimate nature, sticks and stones; instinct, brute i. 476n. *intuition;* unreason, vacuity, brainlessness, mindlessness 450n. *incogitance;* brain injury, brain damage, disordered intellect 503n. *insanity.*

Adj. *mindless,* non-intellectual, unintellectual; animal, vegetable; mineral, the confusion of principles which they exhibit. They will be too often ignorant of what every one knows and takes for granted, of that multitude of small truths which fall upon the mind like dust, impalpable and ever accumulating; they may be unable to converse, they may argue perversely, they may pride themselves on their worst paradoxes or their grossest truisms, they may be full of their own mode of viewing things, unwilling to be put out of their way, slow to enter into the minds of others; — but, with these and whatever other liabilities upon their heads, they are likely to have more thought, more mind, more philosophy, more true enlargement, than those earnest but ill-used persons, who are forced to load their minds with a score of subjects against an examination, who have too much on their hands to indulge themselves in thinking or investigation, who devour premiss and conclusion together with indiscriminate greediness, who hold whole sciences on faith, and commit demonstrations to memory, and who too often, as might be expected, when their period of education is passed, throw up all they have learned in disgust, having gained nothing really by their anxious labours, except perhaps the habit of application.

John Henry Newman, "Knowledge and Education," The Idea of a University, *1852.*

As the nature of any given thing is the aggregate of its powers and properties, so Nature in the abstract is the aggregate of the powers and properties of all things. Nature means the sum of all phenomena, together with the causes which produce them; including not only all that happens, but all that is capable of happening; the unused capabilities of causes being as much a part of the idea of Nature, as those which take effect. Since all phenomena which have been sufficiently examined are found to take place with regularity, each having certain fixed conditions, positive and negative, on the occurrence of which it invariably happens; mankind have been able to ascertain, either by direct observation or by reasoning processes grounded on it, the conditions of the occurrence of many phenomena; and the progress of science mainly consists in ascertaining those conditions. When discovered they can be expressed in general proportions, which are called laws of the particular phenomenon, and also, more generally, Laws of Nature. Thus, the truth that all material objects tend towards one another with a force directly as their masses and inversely as the square of their distance, is a law of Nature. The proposition that air and food are necessary to animal life, if it be as we have good reason to believe, true without exception, is also a law of nature, though the phenomenon of which it is the law is special, and not, like gravitation, universal.

Nature, then, in this its simplest acceptations, is a collective name for all facts, actual and possible: or (to speak more accurately) a name for the mode, partly known to us and partly unknown, in which all things take place. For the word suggests, not so much the multitudinous detail of the phenomena, as the conception which might be formed of their manner of existence as a mental whole, by a mind possessing a complete knowledge of them: to which conception it is the aim of science to raise itself, by successive steps of generalization from experience.

John Stuart Mill, "Nature," Three Essays on Religion, *1874.*

8. The charts of the world which have been drawn up by modern science have thrown into a narrow space the expression of a vast amount of knowledge, but I have never yet seen any one pictorial enough to enable the spectator to imagine the kind of contrast in physical character which exists between Northern and Southern countries. We know the differences in detail, but we have not that broad glance and grasp which would enable us to feel them in their fulness. We know that gentians grow on the Alps, and olives on the Appennines; but we do not enough conceive for ourselves that variegated mosaic of the world's surface which a bird sees in its migration, that difference between the district of the gentian and of the olive which the stork and the swallow see far off, as they lean upon the sirocco wind. Let us, for a moment, try to raise ourselves even above the level of their flight, and imagine the Mediterranean lying beneath us like an irregular lake, and all its ancient promontories sleeping in the sun: here and there an angry spot of thunder, a grey stain of storm, moving upon the burning field; and here and there a fixed wreath of white volcano smoke, surrounded by its circle of ashes; but for the most part a great peacefulness of light, Syria and Greece, Italy and Spain, laid like pieces of a golden pavement into the sea-blue, chased, as we stoop nearer to them, with bossy beaten work of mountain chains, and glowing softly with terraced gardens, and flowers heavy with frankincense, mixed among masses of laurel, and orange, and plumy palm, that abate with their grey-green shadows the burning of the marble rocks, and of the ledges of

porphyry sloping under lucent sand. Then let us pass farther towards the north, until we see the orient colours change gradually into a vast belt of rainy green, where the pastures of Switzerland, and poplar valleys of France, and dark forests of the Danube and Carpathians stretch from the mouths of the Loire to those of the Volga, seen through clefts in grey swirls of rain-cloud and flaky veils of the mist of the brooks,spreading low along the pasture lands: and then, farther north still, to see the earth heave into mighty masses of leaden rock and heathy moor, bordering with a broad waste of gloomy purple that belt of field and wood, and splintering into irregular and grisly islands amidst the northern seas, beaten by storm, and chilled by ice-drift, and tormented by furious pulses of contending tide, until the roots of the last forests fail from among the hill ravines, and the hunger of the north wind bites their peaks into barrenness; and, at last, the wall of ice, durable like iron, sets, deathlike, its white teeth against us out of the polar twilight.

John Ruskin, "The Nature of Gothic," The Stones of Venice, *1853.*

LITERATURE AND SCIENCE

Practical people talk with a smile of Plato and of his absolute ideas; and it is impossible to deny that Plato's ideas do often seem unpractical and unpracticable, and especially when one views them in connexion with the life of a great work-a-day world like the United States. The necessary staple of the life of such a world Plato regards with disdain; handicraft and trade and the working professions he regards with disdain; but what becomes of the life of an industrial modern community if you take handicraft and trade and the working professions out of it! The base mechanic arts and handicrafts, says Plato, bring about a natural weakness of the principle of excellence in a man, so that he cannot govern the ignoble growths in him, but nurses them, and cannot understand fostering any other. Those who exercise such arts and trades, as they have their bodies, he says, marred by their vulgar businesses, so they have their souls, too, bowed and broken by them. And if one of these uncomely people has a mind to seek self-culture and philosophy, Plato compared him to a bald little tinker, who has scraped together money, and has got his release from service, and has had a bath, and bought a new coat, and is rigged out like a bridegroom about to marry the daughter of his master who has fallen into poor and helpless estate.

167

Nor do the working professions fare any better than trade at the hands of Plato. He draws for us an inimitable picture of the working lawyer, and of his life of bondage; he shows how this bondage from his youth up has stunted and warped him, and made him small and crooked of soul, encompassing him with difficulties which he is not man enough to rely on justice and truth as means to encounter, but has recourse, for help out of them, to falsehood and wrong. And so, says Plato, this poor creature is bent and broken, and grows up from boy to man without a particle of soundness in him, although exceedingly smart and clever in his own esteem.

One cannot refuse to admire the artist who draws these pictures. But we say to ourselves that his ideas show the influence of a primitive and obsolete order of things, when the warrior caste and the priestly caste were alone in honour, and the humble work of the world was done by slaves. We have now changed all that; the modern majesty consists in work, as Emerson declares; and in work, we may add, principally of such plain and dusty kind as the work of cultivators of the ground, handicraftsmen, men of trade and business, men of the working professions. Above all is this true in a great industrious community such as that of the United States.

Now education, many people go on to say, is still mainly governed by the ideas of men like Plato, who lived when the warrior caste and the priestly or philosophical class were alone in honour, and the really useful part of the community were slaves. It is an education fitted for persons of leisure in such a community. This education passed from Greece to Rome to the feudal communities of Europe, where also the warrior caste and the priestly caste were alone held in honour, and where the really useful and working part of the community, though not nominally slaves as in the pagan world, were practically not much better off than slaves, and not more seriously regarded. And how absurd it is, people end by saying, to inflict this education upon an industrious modern community, where very few indeed are persons of leisure, and the mass to be considered has not leisure, but is bound, for its own great good, and for the great good of the world at large, to plain labour and to industrial pursuits, and the education in question tends necessarily to make men dissatisfied with these pursuits and unfitted for them!

That is what is said. So far I must defend Plato, as to plead that his view of education and studies is in the general, as it seems to me, sound enough, and fitted for all sorts and conditions of men, whatever their pursuits may be. "An intelligent man," says Plato, "will prize those studies which result in his soul getting soberness, righteousness, and wisdom, and will less value the others." I cannot consider *that* a bad description of the aim of education, and of the motives which should govern us in the hereditary seat in the English House of Lords or for the pork trade in Chicago.

Still I admit that Plato's world was not ours, that his scorn of trade and handicraft is fantastic, that he had no conception of a great industrial community such as that of the United States, and that such a community must and will shape its education to suit its own needs. If the usual education handed down to it from the past does not suit it, it will certainly before long drop this and try another. The usual education in the past has been mainly literary. The question is whether the studies which were long supposed to be the best for all of us are practically the best now; whether others are not better. The tyranny of the past, many think, weighs on us injuriously in the predominance given to letters in education. The question is raised whether, to meet the needs of our modern life, the predominance ought not now to pass from letters to science; and naturally the question is nowhere raised with more energy than here in the United States. The design of abasing what is called "mere literary instruction and education," and of exalting what is called "sound, extensive, and practical scientific knowledge," is, in this intensely modern world of the United States, even more perhaps than in Europe, a very popular design, and makes great and rapid progress.

Matthew Arnold "Literature and Science" Discourses in America, *1884.*

But the people who lived at a distance from the great theatre of political contention could be kept regularly informed of what was passing there only by means of newsletters. To prepare such letters became a calling in London, as it now is among the natives of India. The newswriter rambled from coffee room to coffee room, collecting reports, squeezed himself into the Sessions House at the Old Bailey if there was an interesting trial, nay, perhaps obtained admission to the gallery of Whitehall, and notices how the King and Duke looked. In this way he gathered materials for weekly epistles destined to enlighten some county town or some bench of rustic magistrates. Such were the sources from which the inhabitants of the largest provincial cities, and the great body of the gentry and clergy, learned almost all that they knew of the history of their own time. We must suppose that at Cambridge there were as many persons curious to know what was passing in the world as at almost any place in the kingdom, out of London. Yet at Cambridge, during a great part of the reign of Charles the Second, the Doctors of Laws and the Masters of Arts had no regular supply of news except through the London Gazette. At length the services of one of the collectors of intelligence in the capital were employed. That was a memorable day on which the first newsletter from London was laid on the table of the only coffee room in Cambridge. At the seat of a man of fortune in the country the newsletter was impatiently expected. Within a week after it had arrived it had been thumbed by twenty families. It furnished the neighbouring squires with matter for talk over their October, and the neighbouring rectors with topics for sharp sermons against Whiggery or Popery. Many of these curious journals might doubtless still be detected by a diligant search in the archives of old families. Some are to be found in our public libraries; and one series, which is not the least valuable part of the literary treasures collected by Sir James Mackintosh, will be occasionally quoted in the course of this work.

Thomas Babington Macauley, "England in 1685," History of England, *1855.*

Basic Structures

1. Comparison-contrast. The first sentence suggests the structure with the predicate, *is preferable to*. The second sentence continues the sense of contrast between two types of education. The long final sentence, *They will etc.* is divided with a *but* and follows the division with a series of comparatives.
2. Definition. The passage begins with the main sentence, *Nature . . . is*, which is used elsewhere. In the second sentence, Mill uses *means*, and at the end, *the word suggests.*
3. Description. The paragraphs starts off with references to *charts, pictorial*, and *spectator*. The long metaphorical section uses words like, *here and there, nearer, farther, until.*

170

4. Establishment of a thesis. Arnold begins with a suggestion of argument, *impossible to deny*. The third paragraph suggests refutation with *One cannot . . . but* and *absurd*, and the fourth with *defend*. The last paragraph, beginning with *still*, leads to two sentences, which begin with *The question* and sets forth the thesis.

5. Narration-process. Macauley signals the structure with the verbs, and with the introductory, *To prepare* in the second section. In the rest of the passage there are other references to time: *At length, within a week,* and *still be*.

Exercise 7 (Chapters 4 and 5):
Using the Best Connectors to Show the Pattern of Thought

In each of the following passages a word or phrase has been omitted. The omitted word or phrase indicates the connection between sentences and ideas. First, select a word or phrase that would make the connection clear and, second, indicate the general pattern or patterns of organization in the passage.

1. (a) _____ a truck rolls down a highway, an environmental change occurs. (b) _____ a loaded semi-trailer weighs several tons, the pressure exerted on the road is sufficient to affect the surface and the subsurface. Depending on the nature of the ground underneath the roadbed, (c) _____ may spread beyond the actual road bed and even change the subsurface water patterns. Second, in most cases the truck burns diesel fuel, (d) _____ the exhaust fumes

171

will spread through the air and the vegetation, (e) _____ changes in the flora and fauna of the area. Another (f) _____ of such changes lies in the changes in air pressure and the sound waves produced by machines moving at speeds of over fifty miles per hour.

General organization: _____

_____

_____

2. The Tenebric Molitor's life cycle contains four stages: the egg stage, the larval stage, the pupal stage, and the adult stage. (a) _____ the egg is hatched, the larva emerges in the form that we commonly know as the mealworm. (b) _____ this stage that T. Molitor feeds on many kinds of cereal products such as flour and other forms of grain. (c) _____ as it enters the pupal stage a number of changes takes place. (d) _____ it makes a shell around itself like a cocoon, (e) _____ does not feed or move. The reason for (f) _____ is that the larval tissues are being destroyed and the adult tissues being built up. (g) _____ it emerges from the "cocoon," it is no longer a worm, but a beetle called the Darkling Beetle, (h) _____ it is about three-quarters of an inch long, shiny, and black.

General Organization: _____

_____

_____

3. Some of my experiments were quite curious. In the

course of my reading I had come across a case where, many years ago, some hunters on our Great Plains organized a buffalo hunt for the entertainment of an English earl — that, and to provide some fresh meat for his larder. They had charming sport. They killed seventy-two of those great animals; and ate part of one of them and left the seventy-one to rot. (a) _____ to determine the difference between an anaconda and an earl — if any — I caused seven young calves to be turned into the anaconda's cage. The grateful reptile immediately crushed one of them and swallowed it, (b) _____ lay back satisfied. It showed no further interest in the calves, and no disposition to harm them. I tried this experiment with other anacondas; always with the same result. The fact stood proven (c) _____ the difference between an earl and an anaconda is that the earl is cruel and the anaconda isn't; (d) _____ that the earl wantonly destroys (e) _____ he has no use for, but the anaconda doesn't. This seemed to suggest that the anaconda was not descended from the earl. It (f) _____ seemed to suggest that the earl was descended from the anaconda, (g) _____ had lost a good deal in the transition.

I was aware (h) _____ many men who have accumulated more millions of money than they can ever use have shown a rabid hunger for more, (i) _____ have not scrupled to cheat the ignorant and the helpless out of their poor servings

(j) _____ partially appease that appetite. I furnished a hundred different kinds of wild and tame animals the opportunity to accumulate vast stores of food, (k) _____ none of them would do it. The squirrels and bees and certain birds made accumulations, (l) _____ stopped (m) _____ they had gathered a winter's supply, and could not be persuaded to add to it either honestly or by chicane. (n) _____ to bolster up a tottering reputation the ant pretended to store up supplies, (o) _____ I was not deceived. I know the ant. These experiments convinced me (p) _____ there is this difference between man and the higher animals: he is avaricious and miserly, they are not.

(q) _____ my experiments I convinced myself (r) _____ among the animals man is the only one that harbors insults and injuries, broods over them, waits till a chance offers, then takes revenge. The passion of revenge is unknown to the higher animals.

General Organization: _____

_____

_____

Mark Twain, "The Lowest Animal," The Doomed Human Race, 1904.

Basic Structures:

1. (a) when, as, if
   (b) since, because

(c) the effect, the resulting pressure
(d) and, thus
(e) making
(f) result

Cause – effect. Terms like *since* and *when* signal cause; Terms like the *effect, thus,* and *resulting in* signal effect.

2. (a) when, after
   (b) it is at, it is during
   (c) then, next
   (d) first
   (e) and
   (f) this
   (g) when
   (h) and

Narrative – process. All the blanks can be filled by terms referring to time.

3. (a) in order
   (b) then
   (c) that
   (d) and
   (e) what
   (f) also
   (g) and
   (h) that
   (i) and
   (j) in order to
   (k) but
   (l) but
   (m) when
   (n) In order to
   (o) but
   (p) that
   (q) In the course of
   (r) that

Comparison – contrast. The words omitted and

many that are not omitted refer to a contrast, particularly words like *difference*.

When you next look over one of your own papers, underline the organizational connectives. Do you have a good percentage of sentences connected? Are there some places where it would help to put some connectives in?

Exercise 8 (Chapter 6)
Anaphora and Cataphora

First, pick out all the examples of anaphora and cataphora (not repetitions of nouns and verbs or relatives), second, circle that anaphoric/cataphoric word and the reference, and, third, join them with an arrow running to the reference. Here is an example from the text:

Figure E-4

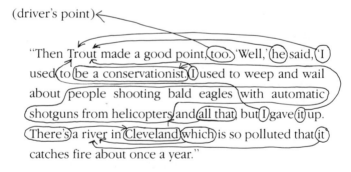

When you have done this check your answers against the Information Sheet that follows.

Text
He [the driver] had a point. The planet was being destroyed by manufacturing processes, and what was being manufactured was lousy, by and large.

Then Trout made a good point too. "Well," he said, "I used to be a conservationist. I used to weep and wail about people shooting bald eagles with automatic shotguns from helicopters and all that, but I gave it up. There's a river in Cleveland which is so polluted that it catches fire about once a year. That used to make me sick, but I laugh about it now. When some tanker accidently dumps its load in the ocean, and kills millions of birds and billions of fish, I say, More power to Standard Oil, or whoever it was that dumped it." Trout raised his arms in celebration. "'Up your ass with Mobil gas,'" he said.

The driver was upset by this. "You're kidding," he said.

"I realized," said Trout, "that God wasn't any conservationist, so for anybody else to be one was sacrilegious and a waste of time. You ever see one of His volcanoes or tornadoes or tidal waves? Anybody ever tell you about the Ice Ages He arranges for every half-million years? How about Dutch Elm disease? There's a nice conservation measure for you. That's God, not man. Just about the time we got our rivers cleaned up, he's probably have the whole galaxy go up like a celluloid collar. That's what the Star of Bethlehem was, you know."

"What was the Star of Bethlehem?" said the driver.

"A whole galaxy going up like a celluloid collar," said Trout.

The driver was impressed. "Come to think about it," he said, "I don't think there's anything about conservation anywhere in the Bible."

"Unless you want to count the story about the Flood," said Trout.

They rode in silence for a while, and then the driver made another good point. He said he knew that his truck was turning the atmosphere into poison gas, and that the planet was being turned into pavement so his truck could go anywhere. "So I'm committing suicide," he said.

"Don't worry about it," said Trout.

Kurt Vonnegut, Jr. Breakfast of Champions *New York: Delacorte Press, 1973 pp. 84–85.*

Information Sheet

	ANAPHORA	REFERENCE
A1	"He"	the driver
A2	"Then"	after the driver had spoken

A3	"too"	driver's first point
A4	"he"	Trout
A5	"and all that"	shooting bald eagles, etc.
A6	"it"	weeping and wailing about dead eagles
A7	"it"	the river
A8	"That"	river so polluted that it catches fire
A9	"it"	DITTO
A10	"its"	some tanker
A11	"whoever it was"	person responsibile if not Standard Oil
A12	"it"	tanker load
A13	"his"	Trout
A14	"he"	Trout
A15	"this"	what Trout said
A16	"he"	the driver
A17	"so"	God is not a conservationist
A18	"anybody else"	anybody who is not God
A19	"one"	conservationist
A20	"His"	God
A21	"You"	the driver
A22	"He"	God
A23	"There's"	Ice Ages and Dutch Elm Disease
A24	"you"	the driver
A25	"That's"	Ice Ages and Dutch Elm Disease
A26	"he'd"	God
A27	"That's"	burning galazy
A28	"you"	the driver
A29	"what?"	That . . . Star of Bethlehem
A30	"he"	the driver
A31	"you"	driver
A32	"they"	Trout and the driver
A33	"then"	after riding in silence

A34	"another"	first good point of driver
A35	"He"	the driver
A36	"he"	the driver
A37	"his"	the driver
A38	"his"	the driver
A39	"so"	truck pollutes — roads being
A40	"he"	the driver
A41	"it"	committing suicide

CATAPHORA		REFERENCE
C1	"There's"	in Cleveland
C2	"whoever it was"	person who dumped oil
C3	"the time"	we got our rivers cleaned up
C4	"it"	fact that there's nothing about conservation in the Bible
C5	"there's"	in the Bible
C6	"anything"	about conservation
C7	"anywhere"	in the Bible
C8	"So"	his truck poisons atmosphere, so he is committing suicide

Next, do the same with one of your compositions. If you have a problem, maybe you need to rewrite the composition. Chances are, your reader would have a problem, too.

Exercise 9 (Chapters 6 and 7):
Selecting Consistent Language

a. Many people went to the old Indian chief with their disputes and problems, because he was the _____ person in the tribe.

(i) cleverest (ii) wisest (iii) smartest

b. The teacher was always pleasant and relaxed, and she was never unkind, but she was very _____ in enforcing school rules.

(i) caustic (ii) harsh (iii) strict

c. John doesn't mind that his girl friend is overweight. He thinks of her as _____.

(i) fat (ii) plump (iii) obese

d. The ballet dancer _____ gracefully into the air.

(i) jumped (ii) hopped (iii) leaped

e. John is a Democrat and Mary is a Republican. Although they have never even come close to quarreling, they once had a _____.

(i) heated argument (ii) strong difference of opinion (iii) bitter dispute

f. After three years of hitchhiking and hopping freights, the runaway youth longed to _____.

(i) travel to his abode (ii) go back home (iii) return to his residence

g. When the machinery of the cell translates DNA information into protein, it needs to be told when to _____ and when to stop. Every message for making a protein begins with a codon, or triplet of chemical symbols, that consists of the "letters" ATG.

(i) start (ii) commence (iii) get going

h. History is not kind to idlers. The time is long past when America's destiny was assured simply by an abundance of natural resources and _____, and by our relative isolation from the malignant problems of older civilizations.

(i) infinite manifestations of indigenous resourcefulness (ii) inexhaustible human enthusiasm (iii) unending spunk of the people

(i) The _____ of operational definitions in the sciences is related to the verifiability principle, and so is the pragmatic criterion of meaning which was _____ in the United States _____ by Charles Sanders Pierce and which was _____ by William James and John Dewey.

(i) use (ii) employment (iii) using

(i) dreamed up (ii) devised (iii) deployed

(i) considerably prior to that (ii) ages before that (iii) much earlier

(i) adopted (ii) stolen (iii) adaptationalized

j. Writers are burdened by physical and psychological _____ that the computer can help them _____.

(i) constraints (ii) handicaps (iii) jitters

(i) become superior to (ii) overcome (iii) beat

Answer Key

a.	ii	h.	ii
b.	iii	i.	i
c.	ii		ii
d.	iii		iii
e.	ii		i
f.	ii	j.	i
g.	i		ii

Exercise 10 (Chapter 6):
Revising for Style and Tone

Below are three versions of the first paragraph of Chapter 1 of this book. The first was the version sent to the editor. The second and third represent a first revision and a second revision.

1. In this volume we hope to help you improve your writing as it affects your study in various subjects you will take. Our research has shown that students can do better if they know the rules of the writing game, and this book is a book of rules and particularly a book of strategies. Probably you already know some of the rules, so parts of this book may seem quite simple. On the other hand, it is often useful to review the rules from time to time; having them firmly strengthens the strategies.

2. We hope this book will help you improve your writing for various subjects you will study in college or the university. Our research has shown that students do better if they know the rules of the writing game; this is a book of rules — and particularly — a book of strategies. Probably you already know some of the rules, so parts of this book may seem quite simple. On the other hand, reviewing rules from time to time is often useful; knowing them well strengthens your ability to apply the strategies.

3. If you're new at the writing game — or at least at the academic writing game — we want to help you learn the specific kinds of writing skills you need to succeed in college or at the university. As you know, any game has both rules and strategies. We've found through research that students do better if they know the rules, and so we've put together a book of rules and strategies. You probably know some of the

rules already, so parts of this book may seem quite simple. On the other hand, reviewing rules from time to time is often useful, and knowing them well strengthens your ability to apply the strategies.

What major changes in tone occur? Does the paragraph become more or less formal? Does the meaning change? Does the focus change? Which version do you like the best? How does the final version on page 1 change the tone and style? Please send your opinion to us in care of the publisher. We will happily answer any comments you might have.

Copyrights and Acknowledgments

The authors are grateful to the following publishers and copyright holders for permission to reprint material in this book:

THE AMERICAN PSYCHOLOGICAL ASSOCIATION: *Reconstruction Recall in Sentences with Alternative Surface Structures* by Katherine Bock and William F. Brewer. Copyright © 1974 by the American Psychological Association. Reprinted by permission of the publisher and author.

ATHENEUM PUBLISHERS. George Steiner, from "The Hollow Miracle," in *Language and Silence: Essays on Language, Literature, and the Inhuman.* Copyright © 1967 by George Steiner. Reprinted by permission of Atheneum Publishers.

BISHOP MUSEUM PRESS. "Medan: The Role of Kinship in an Indonesian City" from *Pacific Port Towns and Cities, A Symposium*, A. Spoehr, Ed. by Edward M. Bruner. Copyright © 1963 by Bishop Museum Press, Honolulu. Reprinted by permission of the publisher.

CAMBRIDGE UNIVERSITY PRESS. *Language and Linguistics: An Introduction* by John Lyons. Copyright © 1981 by Cambridge University Press. Reprinted by permission of the publisher.

DELACORTE PRESS/SEYMOUR LAWRENCE. Excerpted from the book *Breakfast of Champions* by Kurt Vonnegut Jr. Copyright © 1973 by Kurt Vonnegut Jr. Reprinted by permission of Delacorte Press/Seymour Lawrence.

E. P. DUTTON, INC. From *The Pooh Perplex* by Frederick C. Crews. Copyright © 1963 by Frederick C. Crews. Reprinted by permission of the publisher, E. P. Dutton, Inc.

HARCOURT BRACE JOVANOVICH, INC. From *Economics: Principles and Policy*, Second Edition by William J. Baumol and Alan S. Blinder. Copyright © 1982 by Harcourt Brace Jovanovich, Inc. Reprinted by permission of the publisher.

HARVARD UNIVERSITY PRESS. From *Charles Carroll of Carrollton* by Ellen Hart Smith. Copyright © 1942 by Harvard University Press. Reprinted by permission of the publisher.

HOUGHTON MIFFLIN CO. From *Wordsworth* (Riverside Studies in Literature) pp. 110–111 by Carl Woodring. Copyright © 1965 by Houghton Mifflin Company. Reprinted by permission of the publishers.

INTERNATIONAL GLACIOLOGICAL SOCIETY. From the *Journal of Glaciology* Vol. 16, No. 74. Reproduced by permission of the International Glaciological Society.

LONGMAN, GREEN & CO., LTD. From *Original Roget's Thesaurus of English Words and Phrases* edited by Robert A. Dutch. Copyright © 1962 by Longman, Green & Co., Ltd. Reprinted by permission of St. Martin's Press, Inc., New York.

W. W. NORTON & COMPANY, INC. From *The Panda's Thumb* by Stephen Jay Gould. Copyright © 1980 by Stephen Jay Gould. Reprinted by permission of the publisher.

PHAIDON PRESS LIMITED. From *The Story of Art* by E. H. Gombrich. Reprinted by permission of the publisher.

PRENTICE-HALL, INC. From *The Atmosphere: An Introduction to Meteorology* by Frederick K. Lutgens/Edward J. Tarbuck. Copyright © 1979, p. 206. Reprinted by permission of Prentice-Hall, Inc., Englewood Cliffs, N.J.

G. P. PUTNAM. From *The Bestiary* by T. H. White. Reprinted by permission of David Higman Associates Limited.

RANDOM HOUSE. From *American History: A Survey*, Fifth Edition, Volume I: To 1877, by Richard N. Current, T. Harry Williams, and Frank Freidel. Copyright © 1979 by Richard N. Current, T. Harry Williams, and Frank Freidel. Reprinted by permission of Alfred A. Knopf, Inc.

SIMON & SCHUSTER, INC. From *Grammatical Man* by Jeremy Campbell. Copyright © 1982 by Jeremy Campbell. Reprinted by permission of Simon and Schuster, Inc.

THE UNIVERSITY OF CHICAGO PRESS. From *Hamlet and the Philosophy of Literary Criticism* by Morris Wetz. Copyright © 1964. Reprinted by permission of the publisher.

THE UNIVERSITY OF ILLINOIS PRESS. Richard DeFournival, "Advice on Love" from *The Comedy of Eros* by Norman Shapiro. Copyright © 1971 by The University of Illinois Press. Reprinted by permission of the publisher.

Subject Index

Author Index

B 5
C 6
D 7
E 8
F 9
G 0
H 1
I 2
J 3

4
5
6
7
8
9
0
1
2
3